CONFESSIONS
OF A
GOLF SLUT

A MEMOIR OF LIFE,
LOVE,
AND
THE GAME

Susan Fornoff

*Anytime... anywhere...
with anyone... Just
play!. Susan Fornoff*

GottaGoGolf
OAKLAND, CALIFORNIA

Susan Fornoff/GottaGoGolf
susan@GottaGoGolf.com

www.GottaGoGolf.com

Publisher's Note: This is a work of creative nonfiction. The author has changed some names and details to protect the privacy of friends and family.

Cover ©2013 Richard Ayres
Book Layout ©2013 BookDesignTemplates.com

Ordering Information:
Autographed copies and bulk purchases are available via www.GottaGoGolf.com and www.GolfSlut.com.

Confessions of a Golf Slut/ Susan Fornoff. -- 1st ed.
ISBN 978-0-9899540-0-6

Author's Note

It was Lily Tomlin who once said, "You hit the ball onto the fairway, you hit it onto the green, and then you knock it into the hole. So, why, please, the 3,417 books?"

That was several hundred or so golf books ago. Dare I say, probably 95 percent of those books have been written by men, about men, and for men? Doting accounts of golf with sons. Heartbreaking memories of final rounds with fathers. Rollicking tales of smoke-and-Scotch-soaked trips with buddies.

Women account for an estimated 20 percent of golfers. I dedicate Confessions of a Golf Slut *to them. It's time we started catching up on the books.*

Everything that follows is true, as best I can remember it (at an age of never having to say you're sorry because you can't remember why you're apologizing). With the notable exceptions of the Davids and the Sharp Park Business Women's Golf Club, I have changed the names of just about everyone who is not a public figure or very close friend or family member. I also altered some details and chronology.

To my family and friends: I couldn't have done this without you, and I am always here for you.

Unless, of course, I have a tee time.

CONFESSIONS
OF A
GOLF SLUT

CHAPTER ONE

My First Confession

I t was the rare perfect November Sunday for golf, warm and clear and calm, but Marc couldn't play because he was propped up in a hospital bed, connected to machines that made it appear that he was breathing and had a heartbeat.

I couldn't play because I had a small window of time to say goodbye to him, after nearly two years of saying nothing to him. I still loved my ex-husband, always loved him, even more than I loved golf.

And that's saying a lot, because I am a golf slut. In the very best sense of the term.

It's a term that's not about the swing or the score, both of which can disappoint a golf slut repeatedly and she'll still come back for more. Tiger Woods might not want to tee it up with just any old par shooter, but Bob BeerCan and Winnie WineGlass will happily spend five hours pursuing bogey and applauding a stranger's chip-in for double.

It's not about sex either. (Sorry, guys.) "What is Love compared with holing out before your opponent?" wrote the great literary golf slut P.G. Wodehouse. The true golf slut might have to cut short or even pass up a promising date to practice or rest up for a big match, or to keep a standing tee time.

It is a term about passion — passion for the game. As defined by the comedian Tommy Smothers, who used the term oh-so-lovingly to describe his wife, Marcy: "A golf slut will play anywhere, anytime, with anyone."

I felt a little dirty and ashamed when Tommy Smothers said this during an interview for a story I was doing on famous people in love with golf. I couldn't help wondering if he knew he was talking about me too.

But it was a relief to have a name for my affliction.

I hit rock bottom one Memorial Day with a Match.com date I knew I shouldn't have made. The guy listed sarcasm as one of his favorite things; I listed sarcasm as one of my least-favorite things. When we talked on the phone and his dry and bitter sense of humor surfaced, I said, "Listen, I don't really think we are a match. You like sarcasm and I hate sarcasm, and when it comes to communicating, I think that is a deal-breaker."

"Well," he said, "why don't we just play golf?"

Golf slut that I am, I said, "What's better for you, Sunday or Monday?"

We met at the putting green, no instant chemistry, but, so what, I was there for the golf, and we went to the first tee.

His drive sailed a little left, nothing terrible, but I politely asked if he would like a first-tee mulligan — aka a "do-over" — because we had spent no time warming up at the range. You'd think I had just questioned his manhood, because he declined with a gesture like swatting at a fly. My own drive looked like a fly swatted at the first bunker in sight, and when he offered me a mulligan, I brightly said, "Sure!" (It was a recreational round, I was thinking. Little did I know that even though we were not about to become any kind of a match, in his mind we were HAVING a match.)

He made a bogey 5, I birdied for a 3. And as the other gentlemen in our foursome congratulated me on the long putt I had just drained, SarcasmMan picked up his pencil and oh-so-dryly remarked, "How do you score a mulligan birdie?" The polite way, I did not reply, is to have amnesia about the mulligan and quietly write down a 3 and then circle it.

He did get very quiet on the next hole, when he made 6 and I made par-4, and quieter on the par-5 third hole, when he made 7 and I made 5. On the sixth hole I finally got into some trouble, enough so that I picked up my ball and put it in my pocket so as not to delay our foursome. Now he piped up and expressed dismay, not because he was commiserating over my misfortune, but because picking up the ball meant that I recorded only my maximum 8 rather than finishing out the hole with the double-digit score he was hoping would narrow the gap between our totals.

I'd say SarcasmMan was having a sub-par day, except that I'd be misusing a metaphor. When Phil Mickelson is having a sub-par day, he likely could be winning the tournament. In golf, it is good to be under par. The kind of day SarcasmMan was having could not be described as good, not with any metaphor. The guy was just miserable and dragged me down along with him, so when we finished the front nine and he trudged into the clubhouse to fetch a couple of traveling beers, I sat there in the cart thinking that I should go home and...I don't know...get back on Match.com?

But I looked around. Blue sky. Green grass. Sunshine. Birdie possibilities. Aaaahhhh.

The golf slut in me said to the whiner, "You paid your money for 18 holes dammit, now you are going to play every one of them."

At that moment, I realized that perhaps I needed help.

Or maybe I just needed nine more holes.

Well, make that 10 more holes. When we finished playing the 18-hole non-match, I sat down with SarcasmMan at golf's 19th, the watering hole, and had a beer. (Actually, I am pretty sure I had won the drink, and generally I would prefer wine but men prefer beer and so that is what is served at golf courses.) We sipped and chatted, and I learned the true source of his misery: his wife had abruptly left him and taken along their two small children, and he claimed bitterly to have no idea why. I felt sorry for him, because he obviously had some work to do to navigate through the grief-and-anger process. (Men: When you insist that you do not know why your marriage broke up, it is a red flag for potential love partners.)

We walked out together, and then I shook his hand and wished him well with clear finality. He blinked in surprise before I turned away and headed quickly for my car.

I hope that round in 2009 represented the nadir of my golf sluttism. The high point? That's easy: marrying Marc on the seventh tee of the Bodega Harbour Golf Links on May 19, 2000. He was a lefty, so after metaphorically teeing off together with our vows, we synced up our swings and literally teed off together in all our fancy clothes. When the guests asked us to give them another photo op, we did it again. The unforgettable photo showed everyone with their eyes popping and mouths gaping as the shot off my seven-iron headed straight for the hole... GASP... and then rolled on by. Most memorable: the image of my mother in full Tiger Woods fist-pump mode, the long fringe from the sleeve of her pink mother-of-the-bride dress shimmying in the Bodega breeze.

By November 13, 2011, I had packed away all of those wedding photos and done my best to stop sentimentalizing my marriage. It had become my mission to accept that the man I married ultimately chose life with a weed over whatever might be ahead behind Door No. 2, "life with Susan." I was still (and probably always will be) working at forgiving myself for anything and everything that made Door No. 2 so unappealing.

I allowed myself hope someday for a phone call — the rehab Step Eight/Nine, make-amends call received by the loved ones of alcoholics and drug addicts in recovery. Something like, "Suz, I'm on the step I said I'd never take. I said I didn't have a problem, that my only problem was that my wife believed I had a problem. Well, here I am in treatment. Just calling to tell you how sorry I am for everything." Something like that, but not exactly. It's hard to imagine exactly what he would say, because whatever he would say would contradict the beliefs and values that had guided him through his adult life.

Surely Marc would find some words and make that call someday, and, of course, surely I would forgive him.

Not that I would drop everything and remarry him. Golf's mulligan has no standing in the love rulebook; it's a social nicety one player — or Match.com date — offers to another in a casual round, where we just pretend the first shot didn't happen. Yet it did happen, and there's a penalty for this replay, so now we're hitting our third shot and par has become a one-shot fantasy as distant as a hole-in-one.

The other problem with the mulligan: we tend to repeat our golf swing, for better or worse. So chances are pretty good that the second ball will nestle up close to the dreadful resting place the first one found.

Sure, some couples might reunite after a split, pretending nothing happened while learning to do right everything they'd done wrong the first time. More likely, one or both tees off with a new partner and starts a new scorecard, as I had been trying to do. Yet, even as I wrote online profiles looking for new love in the aliases of "GottaGoGolf" and "LetsPlay19," the thought of that imaginary call always filled me with hope. We didn't break up because we didn't love each other, and I wouldn't ever give up hope that such a big-hearted, gentle soul would find peace, and see the world (and maybe me) in a kinder light with his beautiful hazel eyes newly clear. My own eyes would fill up thinking about it, and I would for the thousandth time wish it.

But that's not the call that made me skip out on my tee time that November Sunday. As I pulled onto the freeway I saw my cell phone light up with a call from my parents' home in Baltimore, not the norm early on a Sunday morning. I waited until I had pulled safely into the parking lot at Sharp Park Golf Course, out on the Northern California coast, to listen to the voice-mail. It was from my father.

I should call him back right away, he said on the recording. My family, all back on the East Coast, was okay, he said, but it was important, time was of the essence, and I should call him back. I got out of the car and walked over by the practice putting green, where I could see the cypress trees standing still along the fairways on this pristine morning. The reeds in the wetlands glittered gold under the bright sun, with a clear, cloudless, blue backdrop. Some of the women in my club were already rolling balls at the holes, getting ready for the Turkey Shoot, one of our favorite events.

As I hit the "call back" button on my phone, I thought of my friends back home and got scared. Yet over the pounding of my heart, I could hear my father saying he had gotten a call from a hospital a mere five or six miles from my place in Oakland.

"They asked if Marc was a family member," he said. "I told them he used to be, that he had been married to my daughter. They said something happened to Marc, he was found unconscious at home Friday night, that his heart stopped in the ambulance and they have him on machines until his family can get there to say goodbye."

At this point I blurted, "Oh no!" and started to cry. Marc was 48. A playful, healthy, vigorous 48. How could this have happened?

My father told me that our former neighbor and Marc's best friend at the end had found him and called 911. I remember clearly Dad saying that Marc would not recover, that if he somehow survived, his brain would be damaged. At this I recalled that we had both been so adamant about not using machines to prolong life, we had never written out our directives when we were married. But it did not sound like there was any need for written wishes. Marc's sister was coming from New York to say goodbye, but it was decided that his mother, well into her 80s, would not make the trip from the East Coast. Dad told me the family — Marc's father, I guessed, with whom Marc probably hadn't spoken in much longer than he hadn't spoken to me — said it was okay if I wanted to go see him, but, maybe because I wasn't family anymore, I should go as soon as I could so that I wasn't there when they said their final goodbyes.

And of course I would go, right away. I walked into the clubhouse sobbing and told the other club members what had happened, and then walked away from my tee time.

CHAPTER TWO

Born To Golf, Eventually

G olf was only a "perhaps" on the Mr. Right wish list I pounded out in 1997 to conjure Cupid. I made my 15-point manifesto, typed it onto bright blue paper, folded it many times, and tucked it into my wallet, so that it would always be with me to cast out a magnetic field.

MR. RIGHT

1. He's optimistic and has a positive attitude toward others. His glass is half full, and even when it's empty, he admires the crystal.

2. He's generous, more so emotionally and sexually than materially. Warmth and affection are freely given.

3. He has a positive attitude about commitment, marriage and children. Most likely, he's already been there, done that and figures the experience is only going to make him better at it the next time.

11

4. He's proud of me, and he shows it.

5. We share common interests – perhaps reading, golf, sports, theater, movies, food and wine.

6. He has a good sense of humor, and he likes to laugh — even at himself.

7. He's secure with himself, and he doesn't need to be the center of attention.

8. He has a career he loves, or is working toward one.

9. He strives to grow and improve as a human being — doesn't think he's always right, doesn't say, "This is the way I am, and that's not going to change."

10. He's honest and he's ethical.

11. He's a willing communicator who expresses his wishes and won't shut himself down during an argument.

12. He enjoys sex and has no hang-ups about it.

13. He's athletic and cares about his body but isn't obsessed. Most likely, he orders dessert, with two forks, of course.

14. He can afford necessities and fun, and takes care of such things willingly.

15. He's faithful and dependable. He knows what day it is and can tell time.

Geez, I wasn't asking for much, was I?

Fifteen years later, Mr. Right candidates who were single and available had to meet only three other prerequisites (following an initial attraction): 1. I respect/trust/like him. 2. He respects/trusts/likes me. 3. We're good together.

But back in 1997 a couple of relationship failures made me examine my pattern of previous years. And what I concluded was: I was always waiting for someone to pick me. And if he happened to be married, or unemployed, or depressed, or a party boy, well, at least he picked me! Others might have been under the impression that I was making unwise choices, but that's true only to the extent that I chose not to be the one making choices. Even when in a relationship, I tended not to be the one to raise discussions about marriage and kids because, well, I hadn't been picked for those things yet and I wouldn't consider them until I had been.

I gave all of this a lot of thought and decided to do some picking of my own with my own list. And with Match.com pioneering a vast new world of possibilities, I checked the key boxes (there weren't many in those days, but I required suitors to be unmarried nonsmokers 35 or older), then scripted a cute little online-dating profile full of golf metaphors. "Looking for a partner who has the guts to go for the green…plays the whole 19…generous with mulligans."

Much of it was based on the hope of meeting someone much nicer than the previous boyfriend, the one who angrily ripped up a pair of pants because he had grown too wide to zip them, and who slammed golf clubs at trees or into the ground when he could not execute shots. He became a regular customer at a club repair shop where a group of seniors practiced putts and shot the bull in between business. They'd eyeball ClubSlamMan warily when he stepped through the door, and finally one would ask, "What happened this time?" He always had a story ready about how his club had struck a hidden tree root or found the buried remnant of an ancient gravestone.

What did he tell his tailor about the torn pants, "My girl-friend couldn't wait to get these off me?"

You think maybe I just needed to find a better golfer? I'd agree, except that once my golf shoes came off I felt I had to walk on eggshells, he found so much fault with me. He always spoke glowingly of his mother, and so I particularly remember the day he yelled at me: "You're JUST LIKE MY MOTHER!" I was puzzled, but did not say, "Thank you." I suspected he did not mean my lasagna was as good as hers.

ClubSlamMan deserves some appreciation for enabling my relationship with golf. We went to Maui's Kapalua resort, where I almost broke 100 for the first time. We made social events of all the pro golf tournaments that came to town. On our days off at home, usually weekdays, we would go off on golf outings all around Northern California. These even included my first golf school, with a teacher whose sense of fun had such an impact on me that I still think of one of his tips whenever I am playing in an event with stakes or implications. Okay, I'll share: "spaghetti arms." And, yes, the instructor outlasted the boyfriend.

***

That was my first serious relationship as a golf slut. Although my dad used to take me to the park to fetch golf balls, I did not swing a club until I was in my late 20s. Dad worked in the sugar refinery under the iconic neon "Domino" sign along Baltimore's Inner Harbor and never entertained the notion of joining a country club. None of his friends did either. I don't think he ever even played golf when we were little. There's no way my mother, home all week trying to manage me and my three younger brothers, would have let my father disappear for five hours on a weekend when she usually had fun family outings planned for all of us. And working rotating shifts and accepting overtime to support us had made Dad a hot commodity among us kids, who would beg him not to answer the phone when it rang on his day off. (He always did. And almost always went in, in spite of the chorus of "Aw Dad.")

He had clubs, though, and maybe was already thinking about how he'd spend his retirement years, because now and then he'd recruit me to go down the street to Radecke Park. Radecke had a playground with a kiddie pool where Mom took us to wade in the summers, and a vibrant after-school recreation program where I became the reigning queen of jacks. Beyond all the concrete was a complex of baseball fields, where the thick outfield grass grew ankle-high in the summer, a haven for the bees that would sting me in my teen years when I'd shortcut through there in flip-flops to get to the grown-up pool a couple of blocks farther on.

There was no driving range near us, so Dad would bring

a bag of beat-up balls and a few of his shorter clubs and practice chipping and pitching out of the tall grass. Of course, this meant that the balls landed in the tall grass, which meant that in the years before my nearsightedness got noticed at 11 or 12, I could not find all of them. (We counted. My father the sugar refinery foreman did not put four kids through college by losing golf balls nonchalantly.)

I do not remember my father ever saying, "Here, you try hitting one," and I am not sure how he lured me into this exercise, unless there was an ice cream cone waiting at the end of it all. So my earliest golf memory is purely social, connected with time alone with my father.

My next golf memory is even more social, connected with the most good clean fun that could possibly be had in college.

Well, there was drinking involved, but it was good clean legal drinking that probably kept all of us out of trouble.

Early in my freshman year at the University of Maryland I made the acquaintance of a group of outgoing young men who will forever be known to my dorm friends from Elkton 4 as The Golfers. My dorm mates and I would go to mixers and run into The Golfers. We would have a happy-hour appointment for pitchers of beer at the Vous with The Golfers. And oh my gosh, you should have seen us with The Golfers Saturday night on the dance floor at the Pub.

Some of The Golfers even had golf talent. Bob Boyd — who provided my intro to this merry band by showing romantic interest in me for a week or two — played on the

PGA Tour for several years before leukemia took him at age 55. Terry Boggs succeeded his dad for a while as head pro at Cumberland Country Club in Western Maryland, Bob Darling became head golf pro at Fox Ridge in Maine, and maybe you've heard of Fred Funk, the Maryland Terrapin who's beaten much bigger guys to more than $30 million in career earnings on the PGA and Senior tours, even though he's only 5-foot-8.

Most impressive of all were "the Smittys," Eric and Steve, who often got called onto the stage by the band at the Pub to sing "Brick House." One of them would pull his shirt up to his chest and roll his stomach from top to bottom, a move I've never seen performed elsewhere, even by accomplished belly dancers, strippers, and yogis.

Is it any wonder I associated golf not with elitism, as many people do, but with fun?

None of us girls ever went out to watch these jolly good fellows play golf for the Maryland Terrapins. One of us took a golf class but didn't pursue the game further, maybe because she was not hitting the golf ball any farther. (Grammar note: Golfers do not want to hit the ball further, we want to hit the ball farther. If we are hitting it further, we are still hitting when we would rather be in the hole already.)

Even while sports editor of the *Diamondback*, the school's daily newspaper, my closest encounter with golf amounted to a fierce defense of the use of the word "golfers" in a headline. ("Golf team" had two more counts and did not fit the designated space in that edition.) The nerdy editor had the nerve to declare that one does not golf, therefore one cannot be a golfer. This, despite my dictionarial evidence to the contrary and my own familiarity with that unique group of Maryland students whom I would never describe as "the golf players." I lost that argument but have since won a few over the use of "golf" as a verb, my argument being that if one can be a golfer (the noun for one who plays golf, and a term accepted universally except by a certain nerdy editor) then that must mean that one can golf.

Still, I didn't swing a club in college and knew little about the game. The local golfers I had to interview in my first professional sportswriting job must have been quite amused; I knew so little about golf that I'd write, "His first drive on the fourth hole found the fairway and his second drive on the hole landed in a bunker," until my father said, "Hey Sue, did you know, you only hit driver for the first shot on a hole. After that it might be a three-wood or an iron or some other club, but you only have one drive."

Oh. (Was anybody copy-editing those stories, or did the old fellas at the Baltimore News-American sort of accidentally-on-purpose let the new girl look dumb?) Once I figured that out, I got to cover a bunch of pro golf tournaments, including the U.S. Open won by Jack Nicklaus at Baltusrol in 1980. I was so entranced that humid June day with the back-and-forth duel between Nicklaus and Isao Aoki, I walked all 18 holes inside the ropes with them and got caught up in the crush that surged inside the ropes on the final fairway, while most of the jaded scribes sat huddled around TV screens in the air-conditioned press tent.

When I moved to California in 1985, part of the lure was the fun, gregarious boyfriend who was great at talking me into adventures. So I went on an overnight backpacking trip without a tent, and after finally falling asleep was awakened by the boyfriend screaming a mountain lion away from us. I took a whitewater rafting trip down the Folsom River, with my boyfriend the guide making sure I fell out of the boat on one of the rapids. We visited his mom and her husband in Florida one year, and CanDoMan decided we should all play golf. I remember his mom looking at us both rather suspiciously, asking if I knew how to play. He did the talking, said I'd been on some of the best courses in the world. The next day, without so much as a grip lesson, I could not get a ball airborne. Neither could he, and his mom put a stop to the nonsense after nine holes. We never played again — or went backpacking, or got on another raft. Once I was no longer a beginner at the pursuit *du jour*, CanDoMan's mischievous fun was done ...until he found me a new mountain to climb.

In my 30s, I finally decided to take some golf lessons, with one simple objective: meet men. I had had a crush on a baseball coach who, I'd been told, was an excellent golfer. He always looked so happy after a day on the golf course, I noticed. And I might have thought, well, maybe I'll find one just like him if I take up golf. (He was married and had four kids.) Here's the golf equivalent of what I learned from that strategy: just because you knock the ball six inches from the hole on this par-3, do not assume you will knock the ball into the hole on the next par-3. I never found one just like him.

But I found my golf instructor, Randy, in the local adult-recreation program where I took a beginning six-week golf class with several others, arranged in a semi-circle next to a softball field. I liked Randy's quiet, droll manner so much that I signed up for individual lessons; shorter and smaller than me, he didn't hesitate to get in front of me, take hold of my hands-arms-shoulders, and swing the club for me over and over again until I developed a feel for what I was supposed to do.

Soon, I was ready to step onto a real golf course again. Or, so I thought. Unfortunately, one of the witnesses to my first 18-hole round of golf found the day so memorable, even 20 years later, she wrote her own account. Here, I yield the floor to my long-suffering friend Cheryl:

It was in the spring of 1993 when my good friend Susan Fornoff told me she wanted to start playing golf so she could meet a man. After two weeks of group lessons, she decided she was ready to play a round. I suggested we start out on a pitch 'n' putt course, nine holes, mostly par-3s.

But she would have nothing to do with a little course, she wanted to play the big course. I asked her if she had ever been on a big course and she replied yes. I think she said something like, "Oh yeah, many times."

We recruited my then-husband, John, to make a three-some. We wanted to avoid having a stranger join us. (After all, there's beginner, and then there's BEGIN-NER.)

We made a tee time at the closest course to our home in Benicia, Blue Rock, a nice, walkable course that wasn't too crazy difficult — a great, affordable municipal course where most beginners and hacks could feel pretty comfortable. It was June 24, 1993 — such a big day for Susan, she still celebrates the anniversary.

Trouble started on the first tee when Susan decided to take her first of many "do-overs." Now, the "mulligan" has long been an acceptable courtesy in a friendly game of golf. Golfers are usually GIVEN a mulligan by the other members in the foursome on usually one, maybe two, tee shots — and that is for the entire round!

I guess Susan didn't like the word "mulligan," because she called them "do-overs" all day long. Do-over tee shots, do-over fairway shots, do-over chip shots and do-over putts. It wasn't a super busy day, but we did wave through everyone who caught up with us. There were many rule explanations (ignored!), etiquette explanations (ignored!) and not nearly enough beer consumed. We endured this round of golf alcohol free!

After the first few never-ending holes, I questioned Susan again about her experience on a big golf course. She replied, "I've covered a lot of golf, I've even inter-viewed Jack Nicklaus!" WTF?

But Susan was a trooper — or maybe it was me and

John who were the troopers. I believe we gave up keeping score after the first hole. But Susan finished every single hole. She did not pick up once...no matter how much we begged her to — another reason the day was SO long; good thing we had a morning tee time.

I will say, Susan had a great golf fashion sense from day one! She looked like a seasoned Palm Springs pro. I think the thought of wearing those really cute golf outfits was another reason she decided to take up the game.

The round finally ended and Susan embraced a golf tradition: the 19th hole.

Mission accomplished, she was hooked.

In my defense, I did think we had to keep swatting at the ball until it got into the hole. After all, I had never seen Jack Nicklaus pick up because he had taken too many shots on a hole and was holding up the group behind him. And, I very well may not have known the word "mulligan" at that point, because it was not in use on the PGA or LPGA Tours.

I do remember being on the first hole a very long time.

How did I get so hooked, so quickly? As exercise, golf replaced hiking, my rather solitary pastime, with companionable competition and purpose. And spiritually — complicated and crazy rules and all — it made me a better person.

One of my favorite nonprofits, The First Tee, uses golf to teach youngsters nine values — honesty, integrity, sportsmanship, respect, confidence, responsibility, perseverance, courtesy, judgment — and most golfers could give many examples of how we've applied those values in both life and on course. Golf gave me time to reflect on my surroundings and my place in the world, to connect with strangers and reconnect with my parents, to count my blessings at a time when I was without job and without partner; I have cried on the golf course when no one was looking, and once or twice I may have surrendered early because I felt my swing was so off that it could hurt one of my body parts, but never have I walked away angry. Statistics show that golfers rate higher than the general population in income and education, and I've met CEOs, inventors, engineers, and entrepreneurs through the game. Not to mention bartenders, musicians, and retirees.

Statistics also show there are four men for every woman on the golf course. Even beyond the odds, the game provides a great setting for romance. I had been meeting men in the dark, at nightspots and parties. Now I met them in bright sunshine and we played a game that revealed our characters. Did we count a miss that nobody had seen? Were we sticklers for the rules who expected everyone else to abide by them strictly? Did we call ourselves names when we erred and fall silent when others slipped, or did we give ourselves and each other pep talks?

It didn't matter that I wasn't any good at the game — *au contraire*, at the driving range my ineptness even worked in my favor. Time and again, the man in the next stall could no longer bear to let me to continue to flail away without the offer of a tip on my grip, posture, extension, or swing path. Frankly, many women object to the male tendency to give unsolicited advice. I really only wanted Randy's advice. But I also wanted to meet men. So I practiced saying sweetly, "You know, my mom told me never to take candy or golf tips from strangers." Cue the smile. It always got a laugh.

Not long after that momentous first outing with Cheryl and John, and in keeping with my golf slut calling, I began to venture out to local courses by myself. This was not always fun. Like many board games, golf was designed for foursomes but can be played in twosomes and threesomes. Busy golf courses do not let singles play alone. Quickly I learned that many men do not want to be paired with a woman on a golf course, yet if I asked at the desk if I could play in a foursome that had another woman, I'd hear, "It could be a long wait." One day my neighborhood course called three men who did not know each other and me to the tee; none of them seemed to want to speak to each other or to me even though the course was so busy that we had lots of social time waiting at each tee. I left after six holes, not angry, just bored.

Toward the end of my time with ClubSlamMan, the *San Francisco Examiner* brought me on full-time as a sports copy editor, working nights. In the spring of 1996, I read somewhere about a Bay Area women's golf club full of other working women in my age range that played courses all around the East Bay. Perhaps sensing a breakup, I joined and began entering my scores in a computer for calculation of an official handicap. On an autumn Monday play day with them at Las Positas, a compact yet par-72 layout nestled alongside the freeway in Livermore, I finally broke 100.

Afterward I bought a pitcher of beer and announced my accomplishment, thanking my foursome for their fine company. The milestone had eluded ClubSlamMan, yet when I called to tell him, he mustered grace and said he was sorry he'd missed such a momentous athletic achievement.

But I wasn't likely to play my best golf in his company. I usually felt stress and worry, unsure what was going to upset him and when. I liked the calm and focus that settled over me when I played with these women, who made no demands of me.

It seemed to me that golf could bring out the best me, or at least the real me, and golf with the wrong person brought out an ickier me, or at least someone I did not want to be.

And it occurred to me that I could find a deeper truth by substituting "life" or "love" for the word "golf" in that realization. I wanted to hold that thought for when I started dating again.

CHAPTER THREE

The Anti-ClubSlamMan

Behind every new golfer stands an enabler, someone who knows the game's rules, nuances, and etiquette, and who finds perverse enjoyment — and, let's face it, amusement — in passing it all on to a newbie.

The enabler is not usually the newbie's golf teacher. That guy (and even today with the LPGA cultivating its own teaching division, it's usually a guy) will want nothing to do with you once you leave the driving range and, against his recommendation, venture out onto a real golf course (cuz he thinks you should have 12 more $60 lessons). When it comes to driving a golf cart and flagging down the drink cart and all of the other key components of the golf culture, the newbie must find that special someone who will lead the way, preferably without laughing his or her ass off.

In the game of love, of course, our parents are like the golf teacher, charged with giving us the fundamentals. But do they want to stay around to watch public displays of affection and then get their shoulders all wet when we cry about the breakup?

Hell no! That is one of the reasons why a new couple usually bonds with an established couple. The established couple might represent the new couple's dreams, might even guide the new couple through the hazards of purchasing wedding rings and selecting honeymoon locales. In exchange, the veterans of domestic bliss and maybe boredom either smooch vicariously through the romance of the newbies or have a whole new conversation option, "What does he/she see in her/him and how long must this go on?"

ClubSlamMan and I found our enablers, Rich and Ruby, when we arrived late for our tee time one Thursday afternoon and the golf course starter suggested we join them. They were everything we wanted to be: Rich was rich, and Ruby was a gorgeous redhead. Young retirees on one side or the other of 50, they lived in a beautiful house in a primo neighborhood, yet in one way they probably were more like us than they wanted to be — terrible golfers.

We played a lot of terrible golf together, because ClubSlamMan ran a popular night spot and I worked late nights at the newspaper, so we all had weekdays free. There's the line from the movie *Tin Cup* about golf and sex being the only two things you can enjoy without being good at, later adapted by Tiger Woods, who told one of his sexting lovers that golf and sex were the only two things he cared about. I enjoyed our collectively terrible golf together so much that when ClubSlamMan and I broke up, I thought, "Gee, I'm sure going to miss Rich and Ruby."

And one day when I went out to play by myself, there they were at the first tee where we all first met. Tearfully I told them about the breakup, how I hadn't gotten in touch with them because I figured they were my couple friends, not my individual friends, and we played 18 holes together and promised to keep in touch.

That's how it happened that on the first day of spring in 1997, Ruby and I went out to play at Skywest in Hayward. It's a long, flat course that in those days was known for being a good value despite inexplicable mud patches in fairways even after the dry months. It probably cost us about $20 to play 18, and then we went into the clubhouse to play the 19th, a couple of cheap glasses of wine.

Two of the younger men inside made friendly conversation with us about the Stanford women's basketball team's run in the national tournament, and we all walked out at the same time. One was parked right next to me, and when we chatted a bit more, I remember he took off his sunglasses and I looked up into his eyes and thought, "Wow." Out in the sunlight, they were a mix of gold and green and gray that I had never noticed inside. I guess that might be why, when he told me he played regularly with a men's golf club, I said, "Hmm, men's club. I'm single, maybe I should join a men's club!"

Seriously, I was thinking that this man was obviously a little bit younger than me, and I had seen a pack of cigarettes on the bar next to his beer, but maybe he had a nonsmoking friend my age...And, anyway, I was a golf slut and it seemed the two of us had the same weekdays off...and...

"Why don't we go out and play sometime?" he said.

What could I possibly say to that? How about this: "Sure, here's my number."

He looked down at my scribbling. "Susan," he read. Then those gorgeous eyes looked back at me again. "My name's Marc."

A couple of days later, Marc called to make a golf date for Lake Chabot, an Oakland city course in the hills up above the zoo.

Not a real date, I told myself. He was too young (34, I would learn — five years younger than I was). He smoked. I was having email flirtations with more suitable guys from Match.com. This one and I were just going to play golf.

Then he arrived while I was practicing on the putting green, and walked over and gave me a big smack on the lips. Oh, all righty then!

If you ever play Chabot you should know about two holes before you decide to walk it. One of them is the par-3 ninth hole, which is 134 yards long but all of the yards are downhill on an angle that feels like 90 degrees. The other is the par-6 18th hole. That's right, I said par-6, though most courses are covered in par-4s with an equal number of short par-3s and long par-5s mixed in. Chabot's 18th is 618 yards long (673 from the back tees), downhill at first but finishing with an uphill climb not much less steep than the downhill climb on the ninth.

We would walk Chabot many times together, but that day we decided to ride because cart-inclusive twilight rates had kicked in. I knew Marc, an athletic-looking six-footer, was a much better player than me, a 10-handicapper or so. I was probably closer to a 30, meaning he would have to give me a shot per hole if we played a traditional match. So I proposed "Bingo, Bango, Bongo," a game without handicaps, where the player first on the green gets a point, closest to the pin gets a point, and first in the hole gets a point.

It's a good game for equalizing distances, because unless one of the players is hitting the green in one or two shots, the scoring doesn't begin until both players get close to the green. And in golf, remember, the player who is farthest from the hole hits first. So, say I was 125 yards short of the green after my drive and Marc was 25 yards closer than me: I would get to hit first and have a good chance of getting the "first on the green" point.

Marc, obviously on his best behavior (he thought he was on a date even though I didn't think I was), accepted my offer and we played for 25 cents a point. I think he might have won five quarters from me, but I don't remember.

What I do remember is what a nice, gentle impression Marc made, and how much I learned about him that day. He seemed so well-spoken, and for good reason. Born in New York in 1963 on the same day Elvis would die a few years later (August 16, and wouldn't a numerologist have great fun analyzing his 8-16 with my 2-4), he was adopted by a couple of educators. He did not know who his birth parents were and said he wasn't interested in finding them, because he considered the couple that had adopted him to be his real parents and the only parents he needed.

Marc's father, 40 years older than him, was an artist who had traveled the world on fellowships and grants. I was sorry to hear that Marc, as a result of having had to go on trips with his family, did not like to travel now; he remembered feeling unhappy and out of place as a child, taken away from his friends in peak summertime play season to go to strange places that did not serve Big Macs.

I can't remember why he said his father had decided to move the family to San Francisco in 1978, when Marc was a social, active, hockey-loving 15-year-old in a good private school in upstate New York. His older sister, who also had been adopted, declined to move and remained instead on the East Coast to start her own family.

Marc felt he struggled to fit in at his new private school because he'd arrived after the other boys had bonded; even the athletic teams were hard for him to penetrate. His parents split up soon after the move, and his mother went back east to live, so it was just him and his dad after that. He had gone to college only for an associate degree, much to his father's dismay, and had worked at various telecom companies but was now driving a scrap-metal truck, collecting a daily wage. He had never been married, and told me about only one or two serious relationships in his past.

He was living with a friend not far from the golf course where we had met, in a nice townhouse with two master suites and plenty of amenities — kitchen like new because it was hardly used — and though he seemed awfully intelligent to be driving a truck for a living, he seemed content. He'd start work early in the morning and finish in time to play golf just about every weekday afternoon, and on many Sundays would play with his "men's club." He did not need to make a lot of money, he said, just enough to pay for a nice safe place to live, feed himself, keep a decent car on the road, cover his golf, and, he said, "make sure my partner has what she needs."

I didn't feel I needed to make a lot of money either, or I would not have chosen journalism; I wanted a job I found fun, one that gave me time with friends and family. So though I was sorry Marc hadn't found something he really enjoyed, his lack of ambition did not bother me. And if he smoked any pot that day (I do not remember), I would not have made a connection. Pot made an appearance at lots of parties in Northern California, and one of ClubSlamMan's best friends had been a North Coast grower supporting his family with the crops. Beer seems to be the drug of choice for most golfers, and I often enjoyed one or two on the course because there never seemed to be a wine bar at the turn. So why would I question a hit or two on a joint?

Most important to me, Marc showed no frustration that day over his golf game, and he seldom ever would. He never threw a club, or a fit. His face naturally wore a smile. He seemed so well spoken, nice and well mannered, that by the end of our date, when we sat and had a beer at our cars, I was intrigued. When he gave me a goodbye smooch, I thought of those cartoon kisses where fireworks pop and flowers blossom in the background.

At the very least, the golf slut had found a new enabler. In the weeks and months ahead, we drove north of San Francisco to Novato and played a course that had an elevator to carry golfers from one green up the hill to the next tee. We headed east into the Sierra foothills to Copperopolis, not just because we enjoyed saying "Copperopolis" but because it had Saddle Creek, Northern California's most spectacular new golf course with hardly anyone on it.

A few months after our first date, we made our first weekend getaway, for the wedding of some friends of mine down the coast, and Marc's dance moves were a hit as he fit in easily with my non-golf pals. Though he was younger than I was, we shared a love of 70s disco music, the Beatles, and Sinatra. Neither of us could sing, but we were in harmony.

And for the first time in my adult life, I had a worthy Scrabble opponent. Marc had such great vocabulary and spelling skills, we had to get a Scrabble dictionary and agree to a challenge procedure. (I confess, in the past, I would let misspelled words slide because I did not want to embarrass the fellow who put "E" before "I" because he just didn't know any better. Ugh!) Yes, Marc often won, fair and square.

For once, I didn't feel I had to act less smart than I was. I did not feel I had to act at all. Time passed quickly and happily when we were together. We didn't spend much money because the party was right there at home. No wonder friends commented about how comfortable I seemed when we were together

Rich and Ruby wanted to meet him, so we played golf one day on a Livermore golf course with one lonesome tree and a howling wind. Rich did not take to Marc. I couldn't tell why because they were having their conversations at the back tee, and Marc's eagerness to please me at the time would not allow him to say anything disparaging to me about Rich. I just knew, we were not going to become a foursome.

But the next time Ruby and I sat down for a dinner together after golf, she urged me to be "more realistic" about my love life.

"I see you're having fun, and there's nothing wrong with that," she said. "But be honest with yourself about what it is you really want."

It was clear she was talking about money and wealth. She just couldn't imagine getting involved with a guy who drove a junk truck, no matter how nice he was. So, she could not imagine that for me either.

All I could think about was the relief I always felt when I closed my door behind ClubSlamMan, because I was finally comfortably home alone again. Now I would wear a blissful smile when I closed the door behind Marc, because I was looking forward to next time. What kind of price would she put on that?

I never saw Rich and Ruby again.

Marc and I eventually bonded with our own "established couple," whom we were paired with when I was visiting Copperopolis on assignment. Straight-talking, unpretentious, and comfortably down-to-earth, the Banyons had a perfect unpretentious house with a perfect view overlooking the 17th tee of the perfect unpretentious golf course, Saddle Creek. We'd visit often for an overnight getaway that would include a scrumptious, simple dinner off the grill and a few hands of partner Pinochle.

Their life together was the perfect vision we had for ourselves someday.

CHAPTER FOUR

All Golf,
All The Time

B y the time Marc and I met, I had begun doing a tiny bit of golf writing for my sports editor — on women's golf, which I am sure Mark Soltau will admit he did not care to cover. Soltau, son of a 49ers football legend, covered golf, Stanford football and basketball for the paper, and helped out on the 49ers and other men's sports. He played to a 2 handicap, which meant he was just a handful of strokes short of the PGA Tour stars he covered. (As professionals, Tiger Woods and Jack Nicklaus don't post scores in the USGA handicap system, but they're thought to be "plus" handicappers, as in "plus-6." That's even better than your everyday so-called "scratch" golfer, loosely defined as someone with a handicap of around zero, or, someone who generally shoots par for the course.)

I, on the other hand, was a budding, enthusiastic 30-something handicapper who, let's remember, had taken up golf just four years earlier in order to meet men. Just a year earlier, I had joined a floating club without any home course. In the spring of 1997, I was assigned to write about the growth of recreational golf among women, where I learned from my research about the golfing Queen of Scotland centuries earlier who wasn't allowed on the golf course after her husband died.

Frankly, I wasn't all that shocked. In the early 1990s, I had polled country clubs in my own, progressive (or, as some golfers I would meet later at a fine resort would say, "commie-liberal") San Francisco Bay Area and learned that there were places where wives did not have the same access to tee times that their husbands did. No wonder in 2010, when I was visiting a historic club in Savannah, Georgia, that had few women members, I asked the clueless head professional, "Well why aren't more women joining? Are there limitations on when they can play?"

He shook his head quizzically and said, "No, not really. Only on Saturdays."

I laughed. I worked on Saturdays as a journalist, but most working women have off only on Saturday and Sunday. I had to laugh at the idea that one would join a club where she couldn't play on one of those days. I don't think the club pro got it.

Girls and women continued to embrace golf nonetheless. That spring of 1997, I drove the 90 minutes to Sacramento to cover an LPGA tournament because a local 14-year-old had qualified for the field. She was Natalie Gulbis, who later went on to some fame for that winning-woman combination of golf talent, upbeat personality, and pole-dancer physique.

Soltau handled the rest of the golf, which meant writing a lot about Tiger Woods, until the end of the summer. That's when he decided to leave newspapers for the Internet and a job with CBSSportsline.com covering golf. I waited about five minutes after hearing the news, then went into the sports editor's office and asked as offhandedly as I could manage, "What do I have to do to be considered for that job?"

"I was hoping you'd ask," Glenn Schwarz said.

Like all good managers, Glenn already had a plan, and by the end of September I made my debut writing the Sunday *On Golf* column for a circulation of more than 600,000 and readership likely over 1 million.

This was the year of the Tiger, when a young, black superstar created a golf boom egged on by a prosperous economy. Golf courses filled up and junior programs overflowed. What had been an elitist pursuit transformed into a populist passion and became a front-page story in 1997.

My *On Golf* column had a unique twist befitting the game's unsurpassed participation levels. I wrote it for golfers, not golf fans or TV viewers. So I'd share good yarns I heard, or interview local teachers for bad-weather tips, or review new courses. I gave a shout-out to the lady who played 65 holes at little Aetna Springs, a gem hidden over the mountains on the other side of Napa Valley, on her 65th birthday (shooting 358). I wrote about the mystery of who designed Yosemite's charming nine-hole Wawona temple of trees — and followed readers to the conclusion that it was Walter G. Fovargue, a talented course architect and, alas, not the famous Alister MacKenzie as rumored. I also reported on my first witnessed hole-in-one, in October 1998 by PR professional and friend Jack Wolf on the 12th hole of Santa Rosa's Fountaingrove course. Marc and I were there with him as he then stepped up to the 13th tee and promptly sliced the souvenir into the woods; in *On Golf*, I jokingly implored anyone finding a Top Flite marked with a purple J to please return it to the pro shop. Whenever I played again with someone who had a hole-in-one — at least three more that I recall — I would make sure they immediately stowed the keepsake golf ball safely out of reach of their post-hole-in-one adrenaline surge.

My approach to the column reflected my goal of connecting with readers, and with others in general. The column became a character, kibitzing with fellow golfers every Sunday. There was a tradition for this sort of thing in San Francisco. It was what the great Herb Caen had done with his brand of three-dot journalism, writing for and about all of the hoi polloi and quirky characters who flavored the city. Of course, *On Golf* wasn't that important — it was golf, intended to provide good breakfast company and a fine send-off for the morning 18.

One Sunday, though, it became important. On April 24, 1998, Marc and I set off for a weekday round at Tilden Park, a compact layout winding through the Berkeley hills, not far from the UC Berkeley campus. And while we were on the front nine, we heard shouts from the 11th hole that a man had collapsed. Marc ran to see if he could help, and I found someone with a cell phone to call 911. Not qualified to do any more, we resumed our round, but an emergency helicopter arrived and we couldn't help wondering how the man was doing.

When we finished the 10th hole, we were told we couldn't go any farther at that moment. The man, a 71-year-old having what his friends said was a career day of golf, had died right there on the course and his body had not been removed yet. We sat on a bench for a bit and then Marc said he just couldn't play anymore, so we headed back up the hill to the clubhouse.

A day or two later, I called the club pro to ask if there was anything positive that could result from me writing about what had happened. And she suggested that I talk to the first responder about that. He was the head of the emergency room of a nearby hospital who happened to be golfing that day, heard the shouts, and ran to administer CPR.

The golf course, he said, is the fifth most common heart attack locale. And there is, he said, just a six-minute window for saving a heart attack victim. CPR is risky to administer without knowing the victim's medical history. So why, he wanted to know, were golf courses not equipped and training their staffs for AEDs, commonly known as defibrillators?

The column I wrote about this tragedy was not, I am sure, my most entertaining or best breakfast company. But not long after it appeared, I saw at my own home course in Alameda, an AED encased in a central, accessible location. The GM told me he'd seen a story somewhere (!) that prompted him to install it. And, yes, I was told, it saved lives just about every month.

Covering golf did not generally save lives. But, oh, there were life-transforming issues. A big one in 1997 and 1998, I remember, was whether disabled golfer Casey Martin should be allowed to ride in a cart to play on the PGA Tour. Martin's painful, untreatable Klippel-Trenaunay-Weber Syndrome had caused such a deterioration of his right leg that it was little more than bone and skin. For him, walking not only hurt, it risked serious injury, and doctors recommended he take precautions.

I heard a lot of truly disgraceful analogies. One was, shouldn't 49ers quarterback Joe Montana have been allowed to ride in a cart if it prolonged his NFL career? (You have got to be kidding me.) I also remembered that a male sportswriter many years ago had protested efforts by women sportswriters to be admitted to locker rooms by saying, "That's like saying we should build ramps everywhere just because there are a few paraplegics." And I thought at the time, yes, we should build ramps. And of course we have.

The PGA opposed Martin on the grounds that making an allowance for him would open the floodgates for others with ingrown toenails, so few players sided with Martin. Tiger Woods tentatively, gingerly seemed to support his college teammate; at Stanford, they had roomed together on some golf trips and Tiger had seen up close Martin's withered right leg and the pain that came with it.

Looking back at my early stories, I see that I tried not to take a position. But by June of 1998, when the U.S. Open came to San Francisco's Olympic Club, I went on the record as supporting Martin's cause in the "Ride, Casey, Ride" camp. He had not taken his case to the U.S. Supreme Court yet (the justices ruled 7-2 in his favor three years later) and spectators seemed somewhat divided, but the USGA, which governs the U.S. Open, permitted Martin to ride a lightweight scooter around the course.

He finished 23rd, a big milestone in his career, but I think it meant much more when he returned in 2012, a surprise qualifier for the Open at age 40, and was welcomed back as a hero with applause all around the course. I walked 18 holes with him as he failed by one shot to make the Friday cut, and walked away so moved and powerfully inspired that in the next month, walking 18 with my own Sunday women's club, I would play the best rounds of my life.

On Golf also dealt with slow play, metal spikes, cell phones and bad manners. Looking at the columns now, it's the writer's passion for the game that I see. In our special U.S. Open magazine issue, I wrote an essay about golf's new popularity and Tiger's infusion of the cool factor. "Today, I love golf," I wrote. "It gave me a fantastic job. And I hate golf. It doesn't allow me to bask in the glow of a pro-caliber shot for more than a minute or two before it humiliates me again. I love golf. It has brought me love and friendship. And I hate golf. It takes my time and my money."

(Not sure why the paragraph ended on a downer. Because, maybe you've noticed, I love golf.)

Another piece I wrote in that same issue, *Drive, She Said*, recounted a spring journey to Golf Heaven, Pebble Beach. If you've ever seen the wacky Pro-Am tournament, featuring Bill Murray and a revolving celebrity cast, you've caught the blimp images of the Monterey Peninsula, with whales breaching offshore and otters frolicking outside the course boundary of the seawall. I had gone to the tournament several times as an enchanted spectator, content to spend most of the day in the bleachers alongside 18 with friends, wine, and cheese. Often, it was my birthday. In 1998, just before my 40th, I covered the tournament in perhaps its most disastrous incarnation ever. Somehow the field completed two rounds despite rain before, during and, especially, concluding the scheduled festivities. The pros would have to return in August, at Marc's birthday, to play the required third round that would put the event in the official books. (Never mind the fourth round that year.)

I had always said I'd play Pebble someday. With green fees then at around $300 (now $500!), I figured it would have to be a special day — after I broke 100, maybe. Or when

I turned 40. Those things both had happened, and a Pebble Beach Company executive suggested I not wait any longer. He helped me arrange a visit that spring with three discounted nights at the Inn at Spanish Bay plus free golf for both me and Marc at Pebble, Spyglass, and Spanish Bay. Hey, this was part of my job now! I had to play fantastic golf courses. At Pebble, a caddie we had met through friends escorted us around the layout, which looks completely different from the fairway than it does from the couch. We were struck by how long it took to get around the course, but there are two good reasons for that at Pebble. One is the scenery, the other the difficulty. If the otters and seals don't slow you down, the rough and bunkers will.

I don't remember my triple-digit scores that week, but I do remember feeling out of sorts when we unexpectedly found ourselves playing with a renowned golf instructor. I wasn't swinging the club well and didn't feel up to being evaluated — you know, us women, we won't go to the beauty salon without our hair and makeup done first. I knew I was doing many things wrong, but I wanted to keep my focus outward, on the acclaimed golf courses and the first-class resort and the Monterey Peninsula setting, and not worry about my golf swing. Didn't he have work to do? (I'm sure he thought he was working.) Couldn't he just go away? (I'm sure he wanted to.) Looking back, wow, many students of golf would have paid several hundred dollars for just one hour on the course with this man. I wasted four of them. My self-consciousness about my golf ability was slow to disappear — believe me, now it's long gone and I've become as much lesson slut as golf slut, but I wonder how many self-improvement opportunities I missed out on in those days.

Many opportunities, however, I embraced and was able to share with Marc. We had our first country-club experience with an executive from the regional section of the PGA of America and her husband, on a course called Green Valley. Later in the year, Emmy asked whether we might want to spend our first Christmas together at the Silverado Resort and Country Club, a longtime Napa Valley destination with two golf courses. We did, of course — and on the way played a private course and on the way home played another private course.

Marc and I were not country-club folks. We did not have the money, equipment, or clothes to fit in at most places, but we loved playing with Emmy and Larry and sometimes found a club where we did not feel out of place. I remember a very cold December day where we walked off the 18th hole at the Napa Valley Country Club and into a clubhouse bar where we felt right at home. Otherwise, although of course we did not decline invitations to private clubs because this would mean declining free golf, these did not excite us as much as the opening of a new public-access course.

And this was boom time for golf-course openings. Rooster Run opened early in 1998 in Petaluma, and we were tickled to putt on some of the biggest greens we had seen. A few months later, Wente Vineyards opened a golf course designed by Greg Norman that would become one of my top five in the state. I should add that the property has a top-notch restaurant and a summer concert venue, and Marc and I were guests of the Wentes for dinner with the superintendent, a Bruce Hornsby concert, and many rounds of golf. When golf Hall of Famer Annika Sorenstam decided to make her own wine, she went to the Wentes for the grapes and the expertise.

Unfortunately, I had to decline many invitations because I was still working four late nights on the copy desk unless there was a golf tournament or other story to report. There was no way I could put Monday afternoon's sports section to bed at 3 a.m. and make it to media day at 8 a.m. on a day when I again would have to go in at night to work the desk. Golf writing and sports copy editing really did not coexist happily. I could tell from my vacation habits that I was a natural morning person, and so I reveled in taking a couple of weeks away from the desk to cover the 1998 U.S. Open at San Francisco's famed Olympic Club Lake Course, arriving for the earliest tee-times and writing past dark. That was the week I became a fan of Payne Stewart, whom I had known previously just for his vintage golf attire and knickers. In the press tent after his Friday round, he ought to have been enjoying his chances to win, except that he had just three-putted the 18th green because of an awkward, unplayable hole location on the tilted green. He was only eight feet from the hole, for his first putt. But when his competent try missed the hole, it kept rolling, rolling, rolling, down the hill and nearly off the green. So now he had a 20-footer back up the hill and missed that one. Instead of lamenting the unfairness of it all, Payne told jokes. He described the pin location as "cute, very cute" and held up a little bottle of what he described as drops "to cure that sour taste" he was left with. Oh, one more — he said he was reminded of the putt-putt championships he'd watched on TV that morning. He cared, but had the good sense to recognize the futility of anger.

On Sunday, the golf gods had more tricks in store. Stewart made a good swing and hit a great shot into the middle of the 12th fairway that stopped in a sand divot, a predicament that makes accuracy unlikely on an approach shot, even for the best of players. Earlier, Lee Janzen made a terrible swing and hit his tee shot not so perfectly on No. 5, so waywardly in fact that it landed in a cypress tree. The ball lingered awhile and finally, inexplicably, fell out. I've hit into these trees before and not been so lucky — golf gods have their foibles. But, better to be blessed by the golf gods than by the golf swing: Janzen saved par, Stewart missed the green and bogeyed, Janzen goes on to win.

A year later I'd get to cover the 1999 U.S. Open at North Carolina's Pinehurst, where Stewart shockingly dropped in a long putt for par on 18 to defeat Phil Mickelson. Nice poetry, I thought then. That October, I was playing in a pro-am at my community course when word came that Stewart had died in a freaky plane crash, or maybe when the plane lost pressure well before the crash.

After the Open in 1998, I got back to work on my *On Golf* and nighttime copy editing duties. One of my favorite interviews that summer gave me the story of Corbin Cherry, an Army chaplain who had lost part of his leg in Vietnam in 1969. Lying there bleeding, he thought, this is going to ruin my golf game. But he qualified later for the U.S. Senior Open, and was cheered despite shooting 95 and 90 to miss the cut. The reason I was interviewing him: he had had 15 holes-in-one. We discussed the ridiculousness of the ritual where the person who has a hole-in-one is expected to buy the house drinks — he had insurance for that, he told me. And we vowed we'd play together someday. I hoped to find out his secret. (I did. Keep reading.)

CHAPTER FIVE

Love By The Book

When Marc and I were first dating, I'd spend some time at his house. But both he and his roommate smoked cigarettes and pot, and I just hated the fumes. Finally I 'fessed up to repulsion, and so we began socializing mostly at my one-bedroom, second-floor condo, where Marc would go out on the deck to smoke — and sometimes I'd hear a neighbor say, "Someone is smoking pot."

Between his early-morning work starts and my early-morning finishes, we did not have many late nights or early mornings together and really looked forward to the two afternoons each week we'd spend playing golf and then having dinner. When at home, Marc usually bought pizza or burritos, so he was generous with compliments when I exercised my kitchen skills with much more success than my golf skills. At home, he drank Diet Coke and sometimes beer, but he didn't mind sharing a bottle of wine with me. After dinner we'd usually agree on a movie and Marc would fall asleep, so, after a few agreeable-girlfriend viewings of gangster movies that I was stuck watching as he snored, I advanced us into the realms of romance and noir.

The two movies Marc seemed able to watch again and again — *Forrest Gump* and *Seven*. This contradiction in cinematic composition I tried not to think about too much. I mean, *Forrest Gump* was a feel-good presentation of life lessons, and *Seven* explored the mind of a homicidal psychopath. He also loved *Shrek*, and the *Terminator* movies. Jack Nicholson was his favorite actor, and he often quoted from movie scripts in context with golf. One I'll use forever: "Run, Forrest, run!" for when a golf ball hasn't gotten airborne but is rolling down the fairway.

Which reminds me: we finally had our first fight. We had just met up for an afternoon round of golf in between his job and my job, and teed off on the Alameda North Course. It was one of those times when the club (hey, it wasn't me, it was the club!) would simply not put the ball in the air, from the tee shot, to the fairway wood, to the nine-iron.

Marc walked with me, pleasantly making a suggestion after each failed shot.

"Don't tell me what to do!" I snapped, embarrassed and frustrated at the sudden absence of my swing.

He recoiled, hurt because of course he was only trying to help. We made up somehow during the second hole. I often had to remind myself to be less flippant with him than I was with my friends and family, who were not insensitive but knew me well enough not to take everything I said to heart. Someone else might know I was mad at myself, not them; what Marc saw was a lack of appreciation for coming to my aid. He probably felt like a failure because instead of solving my problem, he thought he had upset me.

But in fact, just that he cared meant everything to me. I felt secure and at home with him, and after a year of dating, I asked if he'd like to move in to my place.

In discussions on co-habitation with previous boyfriends, it had been my stand that living with someone would be the hardest part of marriage for me and I was not going to do it until the deal had been sealed. I had lived alone since my senior year in college, liked it, and thought that while marriage would have its benefits, it was going to be difficult for me to share bed, bathroom, kitchen, and TV, among other things.

Why was I now suggesting it? We got along so well, it made sense. It seemed so natural, I'd curl up next to him and purr. And maybe on some level I figured we wouldn't crowd each other because of our disparate work schedules.

Our 10-year life together began in June of 1998, when I was covering the U.S. Open at the Olympic Club. Marc had a lot of things and I had a small place; we brought in his monstrous TV and cabinet and hung some of his father's artwork on the walls. Most of the rest he stored. When we finally moved into a house three years later, he went to the storage cube to fetch his things and said, dismayed, "What a waste of money. Why did I keep all of this stuff?"

Simple, I said, "So that if things didn't work out between us, you would still have all of it. It was security, which made it worth the money."

People who met Marc found him so personable, they often wondered why he wasn't in sales or marketing. And as he reconnected that year with an old friend, he did begin doing some food shows at farmer's markets. Eventually, Marc went to work for his pal full-time as the company expanded into Northern California warehouse stores, but not before he left his scrap-metal truck-driving job for yet another early-morning driving job with a specialty food company delivering to supermarkets.

Although I did not nag Marc about advancing his career, he loved golf so much that, as I widened my network, I encouraged him to talk to people about possibilities in the industry. There was one golf-course job that interested him, until they called on Super Bowl Sunday, after the big game and all the parties, and asked him to take a drug test the next day. He made up some reason why he couldn't, and the job disappeared. He also applied to caddie at a ritzy resort with a golf course he loved, and after an interview and an online personality test, he was crushed that he was not called back. For someone who had worked in sales, he seemed remarkably sensitive to rejection. I saw his conflicts with others — his Sunday golf group, for instance, after he became president and wanted to make some changes — go unresolved and morph into chips on his shoulder, so that his only way out was to disassociate from his former friends. Ultimately, that also happened with his father, and Marc insisted that it was best they not see each other.

Marc and his father seemed to bring out the worst in each other. A couple of times, we went to dinner together and Marc got up to leave in a huff. I would follow him, apologizing to his father as I went, usually confused about what exactly it was that had upset him because it couldn't have been that harmless remark to the waiter or the humorous jab about my blouse. And of course there was something more. The conflicts were deeply ingrained and over my head, so that I started to work hard before every outing, planning something so perfect that it would make both of them happy. Not that that was possible.

I thought Marc should do his best to cultivate a relationship with his father, if only so that when his father was gone he would not be left with regrets and what-ifs. And he did make that effort until, a few years after our wedding, he finally decided that it was better for everyone that they not see each other. For the next couple of years he tried sending holiday cards and gifts in lieu of making appearances, without response, so he decided why bother with even that. When his sister would visit she tried to get Marc to join them, but I think in the end Marc's only connection to his father was through the original artwork that covered the walls of his tiny apartment.

I always suggested Marc visit his mother back east — especially because we would occasionally visit my family in Baltimore and she was just a few hours' drive away. He always spoke so well of her. But he always said he would rather not, and I did not consider it my duty to exhume all of the family ghosts. Every family has its dysfunctions, right? Marc did not want to talk about his, even when we had counseling together years later.

All was peach-sweet in 1998, and that fall our friend Emmy arranged a "fam" tour of golf on the Northern California coast, with lodging and meals thrown in.

"Really, you can do that?" I said. "Can I bring my friends Cheryl and John?"

Emmy, amenable soul that she is, probably wiped her brow at this. I was, she must have noticed, unclear on the "fam" concept. This is the travel industry's term for a free trip to familiarize media with a property; in exchange for the VIP treatment, the media is then supposed to write glowingly about the destination, not invite all their friends along for a fun time.

I do not think I understood that I was supposed to write about Bodega Bay and its golf course in my *On Golf* column — after all, I had to take time off work to make this trip on my own time — but I did anyway because the setting alone is spectacular. Most of the course is lined with houses, but the ocean is always in view and the barking seals always in earshot. There's one lovable quirk that I know of nowhere else:

two holes were carved right into the coastal marsh, and golf carts are not allowed to mar this natural habitat. So players descend in their carts to the bluff and park near the end of the second of the two holes, then walk over to the tee of the first, either carrying their bags or loading them onto course-supplied walking carts. The first of the two was always a treat for Marc to play, because long hitters have to carry the marsh to reach the fairway, but if they carry too far they'll fly over the green onto the dunes. And risk-takers can fire directly at the green to have a chance for eagle — or, even, a hole-in-one — on this par-4. Short hitters get to play the hole from a tee on the other side of the marsh, so it's really pretty easy for us. No player should resist the temptation to pop atop the dunes and check out the ocean view before putting.

The head pro described the Bodega Harbour Golf Links as "the Pebble Beach of the north," and I could see his marketing point. And this quaint town that had chilled me whenever I had watched Alfred Hitchcock's stark, dark film *The Birds* as a teenage babysitter nurtured a close relationship with the coastal fog, yet it had lively harbor-side seafood dining and a great big beach that commemorated the occasional warm day with a celebration of nature.

I fell in love with Bodega Bay and its golf course, so I tend to forget about the wacky moguls that rise up mid-fairway to create unfriendly bounces on some holes. Oh, and those pot bunkers that are impossible to escape. But fam writers aren't supposed to point out such things anyway when golf, dinner, and lodging all are free. My training in journalism, which generally encourages objectivity, has not allowed me to gush about places I felt I could not recommend, and so at times I needed to summon a form of creative writing to praise the groundskeeper for his conservation techniques (on the bone-dry, brown track that seemed unwatered), or maybe I'd skip all comments on the course if an appealing restaurant overlooked the 18th hole (play here and don't miss the best lentil soup in town!).

Cheryl and John, the witnesses to my first round of golf, did come along to Bodega, as did Emmy and her husband, Larry, and Cori and George. Cori, a petite brunette of Italian descent whose father had developed several Northern California golf clubs, was always on the go doing golf and travel writing for magazines, and George became a wonderful golf course photographer. My birthday was February 4 and Cori's February 7. Marc and I came to love our outings with the two of them. And in Emmy's husband, Larry, Marc had a fellow nice guy who would go outside and smoke with him and make a tee-time to play golf if the two girls were too busy working golf.

Emmy put two couples each in luxury homes right along the Bodega Harbour Golf Links. The one we shared with Cheryl and John had an outdoor hot tub and a big central fireplace, and we wished we were staying longer. The tour included dinner and a tour of the Bodega Bay Lodge and Spa neighboring the course, and then after we finished at Bodega, we headed farther north to visit the 18-hole links at Sea

Ranch and the quaint nine-hole course at Little River Inn.

It was on this trip that Cori and I started talking about writing a book all about golf getaways like the one we were on. Only our guidebook wouldn't cater only to foursomes of men — we'd talk about how the courses played for women as well as men, and what there was to do in the area for families, or for nongolfing spouses, or for couples who wanted to do more than just golf. And we'd actually *write* our book — it wouldn't be merely listings or directory, we'd create yarns about the destinations.

It wasn't long before we had, without an agent, wooed a publisher who agreed to a small advance. So we sat down together to take turns, picking out nine destinations each that we would research in 1999 and write by mid-2000 for a spring 2001 release, *Northern California Golf Getaways.* We could only smile contentedly as the dream of many golfers — to play golf here, there, and everywhere — became our newfound duty to our publisher and our readers. Could there be a better "job"?

CHAPTER SIX

Love On The Links

For Christmas, 1998, Marc and I again drove up to Napa Valley to spend the holiday at Silverado. By now we had begun having matches when we played together, because the USGA handicap system adjusts for men playing against women from different tees. We'd get to the course, go to the computer and figure out our course handicaps from there — maybe a 12 for Marc and a 25 for me, so he'd be giving me shots on the 13 toughest holes. But if Marc, a long hitter, wanted to play from the longest tees on the course and I wanted to play from the shortest, I'd often have to give him back two or three of those strokes. If we played the same tees, on the other hand, these would be rated easier for men than for women and he would have to give me back a stroke or two.

Some men complain about the gender basis for handicaps. "Why am I being penalized for having a penis?" they will ask. In fact, women are being compensated for having breasts, which, unlike the penis, can get in the way of a good golf swing by preventing arm extension and, thus, limiting turn. I know that a CBS broadcaster was fired for making this assertion in 1995, but that's probably only because he, the witty and wonderful Ben Wright, was a man. As a woman, I know that there are times I am at the range practicing some shot or another and I have to make the conscious decision: swing over the boobs or swing under them? It's always a delicate question for the resident instructor, most likely a man who can see the "problem" but cannot relate.

Neither Marc nor I questioned the handicap system. Unlike most players, who guesstimate and negotiate all this, we followed the book — so it is probably not surprising that he won about as many matches as I did, and we often tied. We were perfectly happy about tying if we both played well, less happy when we both sucked. Hardly ever did I whine about how difficult it was for me to have to play against someone who hit the ball so much farther than I did, nor did he bemoan the shorter distances I got to play from the forward tees.

There's no other sport that creates such a fair system for men to play women, and I've always wished the pro golf tours would put some him-her events on television. Wouldn't that get more women interested in watching and playing the game? But the men's tour has been so profitable that it has little incentive to do that. Tiger Woods and friends are not immune to the "who wants to lose to a girl?" school of fear, nor do they want to pass the bucks to their lady friends. Leave it to John Daly, known for his many drinks, many wives, and many talents, to make the astute observation: "The great thing about the handicap is that a guy who can't break 100 can kick the shit out of Phil Mickelson." A girl can too!

For me and Marc, the stakes were not significant — maybe the winner got to choose the movie of the night, name the 19th hole or dinner destination, or (toughest for Marc to surrender) control the remote for the evening. Never money or anything memorable, just a little fun wager to keep things interesting. When we started vacationing every summer north of Lake Tahoe in Plumas County, we'd make a tee time for a different course every day and two last-day tee times at maybe our favorite course anywhere, Whitehawk Ranch, and call the entire circuit "The Plumas Cup." We'd dutifully go to the computer every day to check handicaps and log scores, and we'd trash-talk each other at dinner that night as we plotted our game for the next day on a course that no doubt favored one of us slightly.

"Just think, by this time tomorrow night I'll be celebrating victory."

"If you bring that putting stroke you had today, you'll be buying my celebration."

By our last trip there together, in 2007, everyone at Whitehawk from the drink-cart girl to the marshals knew to ask, "Where does it stand?" and check back with us later for the final tally. One year we tied and considered adding a putting contest but were too exhausted to compete any longer.

We tried so hard to play by the rules, you'd never know the contest had no meaning whatsoever. While many casual golfers will give their ball a little roll or "bump" to improve their lie and make it easier to strike the ball solidly — something even my Sunday club does officially, in deference to the shorthandedness of the crew at our lowly funded municipal course — we adhered to the rulebook commandment to "play it as it lies." And when others might say "that's good" on a three-foot putt, we looked at each other to make sure it really was okay to pick up. Yet just as there was no actual cup, there was nothing substantial ever on the line. Tommy Smothers told Marcy he'd marry her when she broke 100; Marc and I didn't talk much about marriage or the future, other than our next vacation or golf outing, and I did not see a wedding as incentive to achieve a golf score. Of course, maybe that's because I already had broken 90 at Whitehawk and entertained no hope of ever breaking 80.

On the way to Silverado that Christmas Eve, we stopped just outside of Napa to have a little match at the Shakespeare Course, the private side of the vineyard-lined Chardonnay Golf Club. Joe Montana and other ex-49ers had Shakespeare memberships, but not even they were tough enough to be out on this day amid a cold snap that had hardened Northern California's golf courses. Drinking the hot chocolate and brandy recommended by the lady in the turn shack, we could only laugh when our pure shots hit into the frozen greens and shot up like hawks that had descended for their prey and then taken off in search of a resting place. We had no more control over where our balls would land than we would if they were hawks.

We got to Silverado and lit the fire, ordering room service and opening a bottle of champagne. The next morning felt like a white Christmas in California, because the fairways were covered in frost, but we bundled up and played again once it melted. Then we headed home to open our gifts. I told Marc I wanted to give a quick call to my best friend, a mother of two whose marriage was breaking up back in Baltimore, before it got too late, so I went into the bedroom to use the phone. Marc came in once and gave me a funny look, then appeared satisfied, and went back to the living room.

By the time I finished, he had dozed off on the couch, so after a while I got into bed bemoaning the absence of my reliable foot warmer. I found another gift under my pillow, a small, square box with a lavish bow. Puzzled, I opened it. It was a white gold band encasing a row of small diamonds, flanked by yellow gold trim.

Big lump in my throat, I went and tried to wake up my foot warmer. He sort of came around, saw what I had in my hand, and smiled.

"Do you like it?" he asked.

"Oh," I said, "I love it, it's just perfect."

He joked that he had been planning on what to say when he gave it to me and now he wouldn't have to worry about that.

So Marc never proposed, and I never said yes, I just put on the non-ostentatious but gorgeous ring and kept it on. This wasn't something I'd asked for or felt I needed, especially because we had talked about children and he said he did not want to have any. I was 40 now and had accepted that there probably weren't going to be any kids' names on my scorecard of life; however, I was a little surprised to hear that from Marc because he, only 35, seemed to love kids. As we talked about a future that had a lot of golf and leisure, we concluded, "We can't have kids, we are the kids." We could never even have pets, we decided, because doing our jobs and taking care of our home would be enough responsibility for the two of us.

I wondered much later if he did not want to have kids because he would have to curtail and hide his pot smoking. Or because he did not think he could set a good example for them. Or if he instinctively knew he would not be around to watch them grow up.

I also wondered how he could fall asleep when he had an engagement ring to give me! This I chalked up to the rightness and calmness of our relationship, which I seldom discussed with friends or family because it did not seem to require laborious analysis. Of course there would be no anxiety to keep Marc awake, right? Oh, but maybe a little eye-popping excitement would have been nice. At least a question to which he surely knew the answer.

No matter. We were just so content and happy, the first

few months I wore the ring we didn't even talk all that much about a wedding. Then as I began working on my *Northern California Golf Getaway* chapters, we got to thinking that we should have a golf-course wedding.

And we started scouting around and discovered the wedding racket.

At that time, when corporate business kept resorts and hotels hopping, many properties didn't really want weddings. Oh, how they'd cry for one during the recession later, when the corporate business died and people stopped getting married because they couldn't afford the kind of celebration they wanted. But in the good old days of prosperity, they weren't fond of demanding bridezillas and their amateur drinking guests. They'd jack up prices so that the happy couples either looked elsewhere or anteed up so much cash that the reluctant host property could bear to hold its nose all the way to the bank.

I ordered a sales kit from Pebble Beach, and from Wente Vineyards, and other places we'd come to enjoy. Most had rules or minimums that weren't practical for our small party of 50 to 100 guests, and when they heard our idea to finish off the ceremony with an in-unison shot down the fairway of life, some withdrew without even a chuckle.

Silverado was our first choice, and it was there that we played golf with their trail-blazing chef, one of Napa Valley's pioneers in the emphasis on farm-fresh and sustainable ingredients. And a darned good golfer as well. I do think we paid him that day.

The course had a nice setup for what we had in mind — an area near the South Course fifth hole where we could have the ceremony, the tee shot, and the reception. The entire area was outdoors, which could be a problem in Northern California at the off-peak time we'd chosen, May. But the real problem was the distance of the party area from the resort and the kitchen. I had turned Marc into a foodie now, and we wanted to treat our guests to the chef's great cuisine. But we couldn't see how that would be possible outside and so far from the main facilities.

Chef P, bless him, agreed. And the resort's inside party rooms didn't meet our specifications, so we settled on Bodega Bay for our Friday evening wedding and picked out what was then the par-3 seventh tee, now the 16th, for the ceremony. The big, flat teeing areas sat right next to the road and would accommodate chairs that gave guests spectacular ocean views during the ceremony. Then we could tee off to the green down below — another nice photo op.

Of course we would have a golf tournament the day before the ceremony, and a rehearsal dinner that evening in the clubhouse dining room overlooking the ocean. But, with me on TheKnot.com and Googling away, we did go a little bit overboard on the entire golf motif. The trimmings would be traditional though modest — a gorgeous, delicious cake with several flavors (and no golf decorations), a color scheme ranging from pink to purple with flowers on the tables (and no golf decorations), a DJ, and a scrumptious seated dinner in the Whale Room at the Bodega Bay Lodge and Spa (with maybe the 18th green of the golf course in view).

But there would be white chocolate golf balls as the favors. A bagpiper from the birthplace of golf leading guests to the ceremony. The tee shot together after the "I Do's." Instead of the gushy couple kissing when guests tinkled glasses with their silverware, guests would have to sink a putt to get us to kiss.

A promise would be recited in the vows "to play with you as much as I can," with none other than Corbin Cherry, the Vietnam vet with all the holes-in-one, presiding. For some reason, I called him to ask if he knew someone in golf who could marry us, and he said, "I could." It turned out that he was an Army chaplain and a Methodist minister, and so one afternoon we met him at Rooster Run for a round of golf. We saw Cherry, who had 15 holes-in-one at that time, fire shot after shot right at the stick. It was easier to imagine him tallying his 16th hole-in-one sooner rather than later, because he never had a putt longer than 12 feet.

Finally I asked his secret, and he told us.

"I aim at the flag."

Nongolfers laugh at this, because to them it seems obvious, as it did to Thoreau when he supposedly said, "In the long run, men hit only what they aim at." I can't believe Thoreau ended a sentence with a preposition. But I can believe he said something like that, because, he wasn't a golfer.

The rest of us nod at the profundity of "I aim at the flag," though, thinking that it seems so obvious yet we don't do it. We eyeball the bunkers, the slope of the green, the risks of aiming at this side or that side. If there's water in front of the green, we even take out a beat-up golf ball so that we don't lose a good one. We toss grass up into the wind and then finally, we swing away, hoping to steer clear of trouble. Even among better amateurs, it is rare to find one who trains his or her range-finder right on the flag and then plots a shot of that precise yardage to that precise spot.

The life metaphors here abound, don't they? How often do we set a lofty goal for ourselves? Rarely. How many of us set our sights on a certain job, a certain partner, or a number the way the financial planners recommend, and then aim at it? Few.

The last time I checked in with Corbin, he was up to 17 and I had finally had my one. He pointed out that I had now entered an elite club for which only a tiny percentage of golfers qualify, with odds-against at about 3,708 to one. And he remarked that he was looking for his next one. I try to think that way too, although I know I'm more likely to see a playing partner put the ball in the hole.

Marc and I were lucky to see three more together following Jack Wolf's milestone shot at Fountaingrove. One came at the Dragon up in Plumas County, at a small, private media event with the course designer, Robin Nelson, who had yielded to owners who asked him to make their course a formidable challenge to great players, and never mind the rest of us. A young woman in our foursome that day was new to the game, and had those newbie nerves I easily remembered. She struggled to get the ball airborne, but, on the miniature 80-yard 17th hole, so what — the ball rolled all the way from the tee into the cup.

We hooted and hollered, and our hosts supplied champagne for the celebration.

Another came in Alameda at our home course, by a talented college student who joined us as a walk-on and made a beautiful shot after a long wait at the seventh on the North Course. Both 18-hole courses were packed that day, and so we cheered *very* quietly so that the young man did not have to sacrifice his tuition to buy everyone on the premises a drink. We let him buy us a round afterward only so as not to deprive him of the backassward yet traditional celebration ritual.

And on August 9, 2000, at the Preserve in serene Carmel Valley, we saw perhaps the quietest hole-in-one ever. We were privileged to play this ultra-private new course because I knew head professional Chris Pryor from his Pebble Beach days. But nonmembers had to have an escort, and ours was Pryor's eventual successor, then-assistant pro John Pietro, a wonderful golfer who played the back tees. On the second hole, that meant the flag was really too far away to see, at 186 yards with a slight elevation. But when John hit his tee shot and the ball disappeared, Marc swore he heard a slight "tink." He and I rode in our cart to the green and did not see the ball anywhere, so we got the camera in position as John strode up smiling and picked it out of the cup — the first hole-in-one ever on that hole! The Preserve didn't have a clubhouse and hospitality yet, but Chris went and found us a few beers at the end of our round to toast the feat.

I am sure that the spectators who happened to be sitting alongside the sixth hole at Oak Hill for the second round of the 1989 U.S. Open still marvel at having seen four holes-in-one, all struck with seven-irons, in a period of just four hours. But I wouldn't trade our day at the Preserve to see it. How lucky Marc and I were, to have a gorgeous day in California on which to play as guests at a special course — one that architect Tom Fazio said he did not really have to design because it was just out there among the trees and meadows, waiting for tees and greens to be placed — with a talented golfer who had a hole-in-one that meant nothing in terms of competition, scoring or winning, yet made for such a perfect moment in golf time.

CHAPTER SEVEN

Swinging
In Synchronicity

Chatting with the girlfriend of my youngest brother, Bob, years after my wedding, I lamented that the only events likely to bring our entire family together again would be funerals. "Unless," I said with a tease, "you and my brother have a wedding planned."

She, another golf slut, laughed. "Oh no," she said. "Anyway, from everything I've heard, you had the wedding of the century. Nobody could follow that."

Hmm, come to think of it, none of my very nice and nice-looking brothers has had a wedding since that one on May 19, 2000. One got divorced and the other two have been single all of their lives. I must let them know that my golf-wedding-planning services are at their disposal.

Marc's father used to tell him, "I always said I'd pay for you to go to college, and that money's still there for you," as if that would be the moment Marc would throw down his pitching wedge and pick up a Physics textbook. My dad never said he'd set aside money for his only daughter's wedding. My parents never asked for weddings or grandchildren, we never talked much about work at home and they didn't seem to care about how much money we made. They got the four of us through college and then seemed to view us the way they did their daily appointments with the soap opera *As the World Turns* — marveling at the latest twist of the plot and never missing an episode, without any presumption of control over the inevitable hairpins and U-turns. As a result, I did not think it was a big moment to tell my parents we had set a date and Marc certainly did not think of asking for their permission to marry their 42-year-old career bachelorette. When they visited in the summer of 1999 and we took them out to Bodega Bay and told them what we had in mind, my dad started in on the topic of finances and I just shushed him. "Dad, we are taking care of this," I said. "You helped me when I needed it, that was more important."

My parents hosted a pre-wedding welcome reception and Marc's parents sponsored the rehearsal dinner the night before, so it was a nicely balanced family effort. Yet we honestly did not spend a lot of money by wedding standards, probably because we committed serious etiquette violations. We checked the dates with our parents, who were the only people we felt we required there. And after that, we agreed that we would not get pouty or insulted by any "no" RSVPs — no "how could you miss my wedding when I've been to three of yours?" — because we were just going to plan the kind of wedding we would enjoy. We even invited a couple whose marriage was ending. They had separated, they were getting a divorce, but they were such good friends of mine that I wasn't going to invite one or the other and they still were technically married, so we invited them both.

We also didn't worry that our guests would have to spring for $145 hotel rooms, especially if they wanted to play in the tournament the day before the wedding. And as it turned out, the 65 or so guests represented at least nine states plus Tokyo. We didn't worry about whether they would like the food or the cake, because we tasted it first to make sure we would like it. We chose Barry White's upbeat "You're the First, You're the Last, My Everything" for our first dance, and planned old-school '70s music once dinner was over because every Saturday night at home we cranked up the "house party" on KISS-FM and danced; the DJ tried to discourage us because (she didn't say it out loud but she was thinking it) the old people would hate it. Later she said, "Wow, you sure knew your audience."

We just knew we had both been to too many weddings long on pretense and short on joy. So I found a $200 dress I loved at a Jessica McClintock outlet that would not unreasonably restrict my golf swing. We went to see a jeweler friend for simple wedding bands, and even though I told Marc to get the biggest one (!), it was so inexpensive that I said, "Are you sure you don't want something more ornate?" He didn't. I searched out, on sale after the holidays, champagne flutes with the numerals 2000 on them and bought two, joking with Marc that this way we would always re-member how long we had been married. (A year later I was able to buy two more at deep discounts, so we could suffer the inevitable chips and breaks guilt-free.) I invited Debbie and Kristin to be my attendants even though there was only one best man, Marc's boss and golf buddy, Danny, and I told Debbie (shopping in Baltimore) and Kristin (in Tokyo) to wear anything they wanted in the color wheel range of pink to plum. I told my dad I would give myself away, because I had always found repugnant and not the least bit sentimental the idea that a woman belonged to someone and was now going to be given to someone else.

There was absolutely no way I was going to have one of those boring wedding showers, and I have my friends Robin and Kristin to thank for making sure of that. A couple of weeks before the wedding, Robin, Cheryl, Jane, and the best man's wife took me out on the town for a most fun bache-lorette night that included cameo appearances by movie star Rob Schneider at dinner and San Francisco Mayor Willie Brown at the bar afterward. When local lounge singer Bud E Luv made an entrance at the end of the evening, we went home fulfilled — but not before a stop in an adult gift shop. The morning of the wedding, Kristin hosted a lingerie breakfast where I was showered with the most lovely collec-tion of clothing not for golf.

On May 17, 2000, Marc set off for the airport to get his mom. I picked up Debbie at SFO and we made the drive to Bodega. I remember actually thinking of these two hours as a rest, after several days of tying ribbons around boxed chocolate golf balls and slowly printing out my little homemade programs with our vows and the schedule. We had a quiet dinner with my family alongside the waterfront that night and planned to meet at the golf course the next morning for the "Luv at the Links" tournament that Marc had planned, ideally for the two of us to win the couples trophy.

My brother Tom quickly submitted his regrets for golf. Upon arriving at Bodega Bay and eyeballing the proximity of the homes to the fairways, he felt he would respectfully decline to take the chance of broken windows and dented roofs. I thought of Tom a few years later, when Marc stepped to the first tee on one of our anniversaries and pulled his first shot right at a house along the right side of the fairway. Not having had any warm-up, he reloaded and pulled his next shot at the same house. A third shot found the fairway, and when we drove up the cart path to fetch the first two balls, we found an irate homeowner outside waiting to tell Marc, "I think you're playing from the wrong tees."

Marc spontaneously and cheerfully responded, "I think you might have bought the wrong house." The man did not laugh.

Later we learned that this particular fellow had indeed bought the wrong house — he had been seduced by Bodega Bay's stunning scenery on one of its rare windless and clear days, and really hadn't considered that his house was the landing area for right-handed slicers and left-handed pullers off the first tee of a golf course without a practice range.

I believe there is a story in my own family lore about Tom blasting a shot off of one of the Baltimore City courses into someone's car radiator. Thus, his understandable withdrawal from Luv at the Links.

I wore white slacks, shirt, and hat (with veil) and 23 of us set out in the sunshine. And when we arrived at the par-3 sixth, there was Tom sitting out on the patio of the house my family had rented, riffing on his harmonica an off-the-cuff "Golfer's Blues." Then the fabled Bodega Bay wind came up, and we lost a couple of more golfers before heading to the clubhouse for awards — little plastic practice balls for the last-place team, party-store medals for the winners — and dinner. Marc and I had eked out a victory over another couple about to be married, Kathy and Joe, and we posed with the trophy, a heart and golf clubs atop a tall base that said on it "Luv at the Links" and "first annual." (There was never a second annual, we were just not organized enough I guess, and I did not know what to do with that damned trophy after it ended up with me after the divorce. After Marc died, I just knew it had to go and hoped that Goodwill would figure out something good-willed. I did think of the diamond ring my grandmother once gave me, the one inscribed "Jesse to Ellie" with a date in 1943. I always wondered what happened to them, knowing it couldn't have been good if I had the ring. Now somewhere someone might be reading "Marc and Susan" and wondering how the Luv trophy came to be discarded so nonchalantly.)

After the wonderful lingerie breakfast the morning of the big day, there was so much to do — dealing with the vendors, answering calls, setting up the party room, cruising into town for an up-do from a sweet hairdresser I had never met who seemed somewhat awed that I would trust a stranger's vision and hairspray on this big day — that I finally collapsed on the bed to put my feet up for 20 minutes. But the phone was ringing — Marc's mom wanted to know why he wasn't back yet. He and his pals had gone off to play Northwood, a beautiful nine-hole course in the trees just inland from Bodega Bay, and I suppose they didn't stop at just one go-round.

I hadn't told him any time to be back, I had just asked one thing. Because by now I was aware that Marc liked to smoke pot and regularly did smoke pot on the golf course. I noticed that when he did, his eyes would get a bit red and glazed. So I asked him, please not to smoke pot before our wedding, because I wanted to look into his eyes when they were beautiful and clear. He nodded.

If he did smoke pot, I couldn't tell because his eyes were just so bright and happy next time I saw him. With the bagpiper playing, all the guests walked from the party house over to the seventh tee, with my parents bringing up the rear. Then I came out, trying to hold on to my veil as it flapped in the wind. (That veil — my one concession to convention, or at least to my mother, who had expressed disappointment when I wasn't going to wear one.)

Cori's husband George was walking along with me snapping pictures as I was laughing, and then really laughing because as I arrived at the tee all of the guests clapped! Maybe because they were freezing and couldn't wait for the ceremony to be over.

I think I saw Marc say "Wow!" I know that moment when I reached the minister and the wedding party, with my parents and brothers all there in the front row, it was the happiest moment of my life. Even now, looking at the pictures makes me happy. I don't think I have had a happier moment ever, and, I don't need to. It was as perfect as the afternoon of John Pietro's hole-in-one, no need to compare any other moment ever. One will suffice for a lifetime.

As soon as I reached the minister and the wedding party, I took off the veil and handed it over to Debbie. I don't think I saw it again. Hope my mom enjoyed it.

I know she, our guests, and even the neighbors enjoyed the spectacle of the left-handed groom and the right-handed bride swinging in synchronicity after the ceremony. We gingerly made our way down the hill from the white wedding tees to the red forward tees on the elevated seventh hole, a shot of about 120 yards for which I had selected my seven-iron. George and many other guests got great photos of the balls leaving the club face, the strap of my gown slipping off my shoulder in the backswing. Naturally, I had never tried this in heels before. An encore was demanded immediately for photo purposes, and we all watched crazed as my shot nearly went in the hole. Flustered, we completely botched the good-luck third try and then posed for a most amazing group photo of everyone.

We didn't have any mishaps that we knew of. Our divorced friends came together. Everyone praised the hotel and the food, and my hard-to-please Aunt Jean raved about the lemon cake. Aunt Jean was the first to leave when the Saturday Night Dance Party music started, but we've got photos of other guests sweatily boogeying and even dancing on chairs. The back of the program declared: "The bride and groom should surely kiss, but no tinkling of glass can accomplish this. This golfing couple's lips will link for every putt their guests shall sink. P.S. The longer the putt, the longer the kiss." And even the nongolfers gave it a try. I think my mom, with that long fringe hanging off her pink sleeves, sank the longest putt. My dad and I had our own dance, and the DJ found a polka to please the traditionalists.

When we finally got all the gifts to our suite and Marc had handed his tux over for the best man to return, we looked inside our rings for the inscriptions we had chosen. The golf references had finally failed us.

My tiny band had squeezed into it "The first, the last, my everything."

And in Marc's can't-miss-it hunk of gold? One word from the professional journalist: "Meow."

CHAPTER EIGHT

Merger And Merger

Any kind of a golf nut might think she can guess where we went on our honeymoon. St. Andrews, the birthplace of golf, yes? Wouldn't we be roaming Scotland, consulting with caddies we couldn't understand while swilling Scotch we couldn't stomach??? Mmmmm.

For some time, that's where we thought we should go. But Marc, non-jetsetter that he was, seemed unexcited. Golf honeymoon? Yes, he was on board for that. Many hours on a plane (perhaps in some discomfort without cigarette or joint) didn't float his boat. And the more I, the designated planner, looked into it — the often-nasty weather, the exorbitant green fees, the difficulty of securing tee times, and, oh, the unwelcome mat to women by some of the most elite clubs there — the less convinced I became that our marriage required the blessing of the Church of Scotland.

For the most part, I was too tired to go hunting for golf balls in the gobbling gorse. Throughout 1999 I had been researching *Northern California Golf Getaways,* traveling whenever I could fit a jaunt into my work schedule. And in August of that year, my newspaper's owner announced it was buying the big morning paper next door, the *San Francisco Chronicle,* and merging the two. It wasn't going to happen that day or that month, of course — just far enough off in 2000 that both staffs would all be stressfully speculating for months to come.

The *Chronicle* already had its own perfectly capable golf writer in Pat Sullivan. And though it quickly became known that Glenn Schwarz would be in command of the two staffs, I knew my boss was not going to be able to pick his people over their people in every position. I also knew that I was a newlywed who wanted to stay close to home and not work so many late nights. Maybe with the merger I could move to another department — one of the weekly or Sunday feature sections focused on lifestyle, travel, and recreation.

I thought 2000 might be my last year writing golf, so I pleaded to cover the Masters Tournament, usually a plum assignment for columnists at the paper. "Just once, I'll never ask again," I told my boss. What could Glenn say? He was invited to my wedding! But having had my "just once," I cannot imagine that journalists beg for this assignment. Reached via a nearly three-hour drive from Atlanta's Hartsfield airport, Augusta is a tired Georgia city, with limited lodging properties that justify tripling their usual rates the week of the Masters by buying new beddings the week before. Any good restaurants are booked up months before the tournament, by those in the know.

It is only when a golf slut roams the grounds of Alister MacKenzie's Augusta National that the event's appeal bubbles over. There are the magnolias, yes, and the blindingly white bunkers. But the Committee, in the green jackets (and in those days all men), puts a cap on ticket sales and controls spectator behavior to such an extent that if one does not behave, one does not get a badge the next year. It also gives the media a lot of love, from facilities to food, and I loved the golf course from 1 to 18 for four days running. Even at 42, I wanted to walk the tournament the way I had walked the U.S. Open at 22, and the sloping terrain stunned me. I didn't realize that when Jim Nantz said "down at Amen Corner" he meant a steep downhill walk that would require, eventually, a steep uphill walk. On Saturday morning, halfway through the four-day trek, I slipped out to a local department store to buy new sneakers. Of course, I conserved enough energy to play the course on Monday if my number was selected in the media lottery for a tee time, but the back-room selection process did not go my way. That's probably a good thing, considering that we most likely would have been playing from the same distance the pros had played from a day earlier. Maybe the back-room selection committee knew I would have complained my way all around the hallowed grounds.

In June, I would be covering the U.S. Open again, another physically grueling assignment because it was at Pebble Beach. Pebble does not have the ski runs of Augusta, but what it does have is a layout where holes are not adjacent and the turn is not at the clubhouse. Typically, a golf course has nine holes on one side of the clubhouse, and then golfers have a quick intermission after nine to use the rest room and replenish the cooler. The other nine then go back out away from the clubhouse and return, with the clubhouse perched above the 18th green. So typically, the first and 10th tees and ninth and 18th greens neighbor the clubhouse. At Pebble, No. 1 leaves the Lodge. And the golfer returns to the Lodge only after finishing play on 18 and climbing the stairs to the Tap Room, one of those renowned bars of golf lore.

Pebble's layout makes for a gorgeous golf experience but a challenging golf viewing experience. And for the U.S. Open, the media center was not in the Lodge but several hundred yards beyond it. If you wanted to be a responsible reporter and go out and watch some of the golf, you were going to be a tired reporter. That was me. I was so tired, I cannot remember where I bunked during that U.S. Open. I attended subsequent U.S. Opens as a spectator — memorably, 2010 at Pebble — and they are much easier to watch when not working. When you get tired, you just head for the big hospitality tent with the big screen TVs and order up a Bloody Mary! That is the life.

Pebble Beach might have made for an ideal golf honeymoon, except that this was May and the U.S. Open was coming in June, and I was about to be wrapped up in previews and coverage. And during my previous explorations of the

Monterey Peninsula, almost as beloved among golfers as the birthplace of golf, I had discovered the sunny side of area golf, on the other side of Highway 1, in Carmel Valley. So Marc and I booked six nights at the Carmel Valley Ranch, with easy access to our favorite golf courses in the area, yet also with sure sunshine even when the coast might be fogged in.

We played the resort's billy-goat course designed by Pete Dye, and had a round at rugged, links-style Spanish Bay, and another at historic Pasatiempo, designed by the same Alister MacKenzie who was responsible for Augusta National.

We also played Poppy Hills, a course in the forest ridiculed by some for its big, undulating greens, but one that we loved — maybe for its big, undulating greens.

But the round I remember best: it was late on a Saturday afternoon and Old Del Monte in Monterey had a twilight special known mostly to locals. So this course that cost $100 to play, or more, cost us only $20 each as we finished in the dusk on a warm evening.

It seemed like such a great way to spend a honeymoon, I don't think I realized we were not the norm until a couple of months later, when I would interview eight golfing couples for an article for the USGA's *Golf Journal*. The conservative publication deleted any references to "golf sluts" that Tommy Smothers might have made in talking about his wife's love for the game. But *Golf Journal* did allow for a deeper look at couples golf than "I just play with her so she won't spend five hours shopping."

One of the couples, elderly and long-married, loved golf and each other, but didn't particularly love playing golf together. The husband, an accomplished player, had pissed off the wife irreconcilably one day when, after his morning 18, he offered to walk along with her for her round. She thought this quite companionable of him, except that he brought his putter and began putting alongside her, rolling his ball along yet advancing it much better than she was by swinging fully with her driver, fairway wood, seven-iron and wedge. I believe our interview was 40 years later and she still hadn't gotten over the perceived insult. (To his credit, he admitted, to me, "I probably shouldn't have done it.")

In a couple of cases, the husbands had really wanted their wives to take up golf, and had encouraged them to such an extent that the wives became better than the husbands were.

Did the men then allow their wives to give them strokes to equalize their matches? Oh no.

One of the things I learned in researching the story was that while 25 percent of women who golf say they really enjoy playing with their husbands, not even 5 percent of the men say they enjoy playing with their wives. I am not sure if this was a statistical glitch created by the fact that more husbands of golfing women play the game than wives of golfing men play the game. Or, if the husbands I interviewed all claimed to enjoy playing golf with their wives because I was not doing an anonymous survey and whatever they said would appear in print, attributed to them.

The only part of golf with Marc that I did not like was the ride to the golf course. The longer we were together, the freer he felt to speed, tailgate and lane-change. A lover of NASCAR, he felt confident behind the wheel. But it made me nervous as a passenger — and even more nervous on the rare occasions I drove, because I could just feel him there next to me wanting me to go faster, close the gap, and move on over into the lane that was moving more swiftly along at that moment.

Once we arrived at the golf course, hopefully with time to take a few deep breaths, we co-existed harmoniously. We did not have arguments on the golf course, and often we were able to discuss things, sitting or walking side by side rather than gazing at each other over the dinner table, that had been troubling us. There hadn't been anyone I enjoyed playing golf with more than I enjoyed playing with Marc, and early in our marriage we did our best to have two days off together every week when we could have a leisurely morning and then get out on a golf course somewhere. During this time, Marc would work for a few hours on Thursdays before his regular afternoon golf league, and then work long days Fridays, Saturdays and Sundays. He'd play golf with me on Monday and sometimes Tuesday, then on Wednesday would drive out to the Central Valley to marshal and play golf, dawn to dusk, at a two-course complex called Diablo Grande. We weren't living to work, we were working to golf.

A relationship expert I interviewed while doing my USGA story suggested that couples brainstorm together about making their golf together more intimate. He suggested sneaking along a picnic basket and then dropping off the course for some romantic time under a tree somewhere. Marc and I thought this was hilarious. What, in the middle of a round? You've just birdied and gotten some momentum, or you've just triple-bogeyed and need to get over it. Plus, the course is packed, and you're just going to give up your spot? Ha. We had the rest of the day together, and this sacred shared experience would create all the romance we needed and wanted — later.

The time came, finally, when I asked my husband if it would be okay with him if I didn't cover golf anymore. I already knew the answer, because I didn't cover golf when I met him and that didn't curtail the courtship. Someone else I might have thought I had impressed with my golf writer status — maybe he'd want a divorce from the home and garden writer. Not Marc, though. We were living an idyllic life, we had even gotten a DVR so that we could pause the TV and have a conversation without missing a NASCAR lap or PGA Tour putt. And if we were never invited to another country club, so what, we could get a $90 monthly resident's card and play all the golf we wanted on weekdays at our local course.

The day our new bed arrived, I remember lying back on it and thinking, "Ahhh. Marc has a job he likes, I have a job I like, we have a house and a new bed. We love each other.

We play golf together a couple of times a week. I've even broken 90. Life is perfect."

Within just three years of the merger, the newspaper industry had begun to lose readers to the Internet, and contraction was beginning in the newsroom. I had been through five jobs at the *Chronicle* and grew so disenchanted with the business that I went to school at night to earn a paralegal certificate. Marc came to graduation with me and seemed proud. If he thought I had wasted my time or our money, he never told me so.

At the same time, the food marketing business took a tumble and he was unemployed for a stretch.

We were not rich and did not have emergency savings, but we could cover the monthly bills. So I suggested he use the time to chart his own course and find something he would enjoy doing. I envisioned him putting aside his pot so that he could pass a drug test, and spending hours every day on the computer looking for prospects.

Instead, I saw him playing golf just about every day. So, in addition to working my regular job, freelancing, going to school, and doing my assignments, I'd search the job listings for Marc. Sometimes a job possibility would excite him, until he found out the company drug-tested prospects. I tried once or twice to talk to him about this, to urge him to take a couple of months off pot so he could pass. We did not argue. He simply ignored me, and I did not press. The two sales jobs that he did take on turned out to be for disreputable companies that he was ultimately embarrassed to be representing. If only one of us had done a little upfront research. Marc optimistically did not, and his more cynical wife did not think it was her place.

I really did not know what to do at this point. I knew I was not marrying a Fortune 500 executive, but I expected Marc to work without having to ask it of him, certainly without demanding it of him. So when he didn't, my ideas of what it meant to be a supportive friend and wife began to waver in the face of fear.

On the golf course, I had cultivated a fearless attitude by doing something many players consider to be a jinx: adding up my score late in the round to see what I needed to do to break net par, or 90, or 100. The "don't tell me" school of thought is so prevalent, especially among women, that when I add up scores at the turn I will ask my companions, "Do you want to know?" before I announce them. Later I even came across an LPGA player who refused to look at the scoreboard because it made her nervous; I believe she lost one event because she did not know she needed only to par the last hole to make it into a playoff, instead working herself into a bundle of nerves trying so desperately to make birdie that she ended up with bogey.

I liked adding a little pressure on the final hole. It gave me a taste of the pro tournaments I would never enter when I told Marc on the 18th green at Blue Rock Springs, "If I can make this putt, that's an 89." Then when I made it, we had something to celebrate together that was utterly insignificant to the rest of the world but full of joy for us.

"You have to look your fears in the eye," I told that LPGA youngster, who had heard the same thing from a Hall of Famer.

But it was not so easy away from the golf course, with real-life fears about our livelihood. Was I going to have to carry us? Could I? And finally, the question I least wanted to ask myself, did I want to?

I think this was when I started feeling a little nervous.

CHAPTER NINE

My Swing Flaw

A golf swing is like a personality, the sum of many abilities, components, quirks, and limitations. Some of these result from DNA, some from upbringing, some from experience. Flaws can be overcome, of course, but first we have to recognize them as flaws. Then, ideally, we find a coach who communicates effectively with the expertise to help us improve.

I'm betting if you ask Tiger Woods, Annika Sorenstam, or anybody in the Hall of Fame, every golfer has that one nagging swing flaw that creeps back into the game just when they think they have mastered it. And often it's that one characteristic swing flaw that's to blame for some sudden fault we think is another matter entirely. My swing flaw has to do with the plane on which the club travels. Once, I went to an instructor for help with my chipping. I was happy with my distance off the tee and in the fairway, but I was having trouble with the third and fourth shots. Did he usher me directly to the chipping practice area? No, we went to the driving range where his camera showed just how far off plane my swing had diverted. After a little work there, the chipping came easy.

But of course you can't walk around obsessing about your swing flaw and expect to be successful when you step out onto the golf course. The day after that lesson at the Kapalua Golf Academy, I enjoyed one of the most memorable rounds of golf in my life, with three women who regularly play the Plantation course that Ben Crenshaw and Bill Coore had designed to fiercely guard par. Built high on Maui, with lots of ball-gobbling ravines and shot-steering winds, the Plantation forces golfers to forget to look around and marvel at the ocean views. Pods of whales have made shows of spouts offshore without anyone to applaud because the potential spectators were busy keeping their heads down and still over the golf ball.

I had played here once (with ClubSlamMan) and couldn't keep track of my putts, much less my score. On this day, I started off in the same golf horror genre, losing a ball in a barranca on the first hole.

"What is going on?" I asked myself, doing a quick check-up on my swing thoughts.

Aha! I realized that my brain was full of yesterday's information, and instead of aiming at the target I was trying to mold my swing in accordance with the lesson I'd had the day before.

Not good.

Obsessing to correct my flaw was interfering with my

natural ability. Once I told myself, "That's something you need to work on at the range, not here on the course," I let my swing be my swing and turned my attention to strategies that would help my score — especially, listening to my expert companions on putt speed and break. I did not break 100 but came close enough to think that I would next time. In the meantime, I would have to head for the range periodically to minimize the effect of that flaw, because the more often I play golf without paying it heed, the more likely it would creep back in and wreak havoc with my game in ways I may not recognize.

If only driving range practice would overcome my personality flaw. If you don't like me, you'd say that I am a know-it-all who won't keep her mouth shut. If you do like me, you might describe me instead as an honest go-getter. Let's settle on something in the middle: I'm a know-it-all who doesn't sit quietly.

Sometimes, this is a beautiful thing. It moved me to help form the Association for Women in Sports Media, and to urge *USA Today* to get the NFL to create equal-access policies for women sportswriters. It branded me as a planner among friends and family, so that they expect me to instigate outings with the expectation of ensuing fun.

It has even helped people.

One day I was in line at the pharmacy, and a very old woman a few heads in front of me was having a prescription filled. The pharmacist was asking her if she would like a generic.

Speaking loudly so she could hear, he told her, "You'll save $70 with the generic." She was nervous, not sure she should make the money-saving choice over what her almighty doctor had written down.

So I said firmly, "You want the generic, it's the same thing but with a different name and package, and it's a lot less expensive."

And everyone in line nodded and uh-huh'd. She looked at all of us, said, "Oh, okay," and took the generic.

When I got to the window, the pharmacist said, "Now I know I should be a little more forceful."

My eyes filled with tears as I walked away, because it seemed I was always fighting that impulse to be forceful. That's how I had just helped an elderly woman save $70, yet that's also how I tick off a lot of people. Especially men. I get that they can't help thinking that they are supposed to be stronger than me and smarter than me, that they think they're supposed to take care of me. But I was the oldest of four, and even though my siblings are all men now, I was charged with taking care of them when Mom and Dad got a night out. I was also an A student with a lot expected of me. I'm right more often than I'm wrong. My parents either forgot or decided not to tell me I would be wise to seem less sure of myself around men.

I know a lot of women who are the same, but they don't struggle with men the way that I do. I'm too "bossy," a derogatory term oddly reserved for overly assertive women and never used to describe a man. Other women speak in soft, feminine, "well, I'm not sure, but..." tones that endear them to the fiercer sex and, dare I say, help them get their way.

They're smarter than me. When Al Gore was in San Francisco the day before he was expected to win the Nobel Peace Prize, I represented my section in the daily editorial meeting, where top editors sit around a big conference table to decide which stories would have the biggest play the next day. I thought for sure the Gore story would make the front page, and my manager made a case for it. Oddly, the room turned up its collective nose.

Me? I sat quietly, the travel editor at the time, no expert on news decisions.

My manager, the top-ranking woman editor on the masthead, didn't give up. As the conversation continued, she said without excess conviction or force, "I really think this is a front-page story for us. He's well liked in San Francisco and for him to be here when he wins the Nobel Peace Prize is something that will be of great interest to our readers." The other editors listed several other pieces for consideration for the front page. And just as everyone was leaving the room, my supervisor made another remark lightly that we shouldn't overlook the Gore story.

She sounded a little like a golf instructor giving a lesson to an 80-year-old — not making her case louder or more forceful, just lightly, quietly tossing up one or two points and hoping they made a graceful landing.

Later, I expressed awe and admiration for her delivery, which, I saw when I unrolled the paper the next morning, proved successful. "I could use lessons," I told her.

I think she laughed. Really, I was no more likely to make my points in a soft, feminine voice than I was to drive a golf ball 300 yards. I was better off acknowledging this flaw and hoping that others could overlook it.

In my early days at the newspaper, I had talked to my sports editor about my take-charge attitude.

"What do I do about it?"

Glenn shrugged. "Play sports?"

So, golf. Which had its own trials and tribulations related to tone of voice. When my friend Buffy and I entered Oakland's first four-ball championship — weird name for a golf format for two-person teams, with each team's best ball counting on each hole — we thought we were entering the women's flight, and we weren't sure our handicaps (20ish and 25ish) even qualified. On the first day of the two-day event, we were paired with two men, because, we learned, no other women had entered. The field was small, so there were no separate flights and Buffy and I got to play from the forward tees, with seniors at the next tees and non-senior men at the third set of tees. We both played lights-out the first day, well below our handicaps, and went out the second day with the second-place pair, which was trailing us by seven shots. Some of the men, we knew, were grumbling about all of the strokes we were getting and the advantage we had playing from the forward tees.

We appeased them on the second day, when both of us experienced a U-turn in fortunes with the same clubs that had been so good to us a day earlier. Our companions both birdied the first hole for a net eagle, and we figured we were in trouble. At the sixth hole, one of the men was on the green in regulation, putting for another birdie that would go on the card as an eagle because he got a stroke. The other was in the bushes behind the green in three. When I arrived at the green, the two were dropping a ball alongside the green and the one who had gone in the bushes was quickly chipping it. It was a move so outside the rules, I just said quizzically, "What are you doing?"

The one putting for birdie answered, "Unplayable lie, line of flight relief."

I just wrinkled my nose and shook my head, so fictional was this reasoning. (The options for relief from an unplayable lie — and we've all had one of these, haven't we? — do not anywhere include the words "line of flight.")

TroubleMan had other options, but, who cares, his partner was putting for birdie and his ball wasn't going to count anyway. He silently picked up, and his partner made par for a net birdie.

On the next hole, a par-3, TroubleMan hit his tee shot toward an environmental area that was not in play. He called Buffy over.

"I think this is in play but I thought I should ask, since your partner called me for a penalty on the last hole."

She eyeballed his predicament as conscientiously as she

would if it were hers.

"If it were me, I would say that it's not in play."

He threw up his arms, picked up the ball (without asking for another opinion) and went back 40 yards to play another shot. He did not speak to us again and repeatedly would hit his ball out of play and go walking off to leave his partner to finish the hole.

Buffy and I naturally were put off by all of this. She fretted over what she had done wrong there — maybe his ball was in play, she wasn't a rules official, she thought he was just asking for her opinion and would ask for someone else's if he had any question. And I wondered how my wrinkled nose had been interpreted as calling a penalty. I guess I just sounded like enough of an authoritative know-it-all to be believed — and, by TroubleMan, despised.

Of course, here's what you really want to know: Buffy and I did not completely hate each other by the end of the day, and, despite our disastrous turnaround, we even won the tournament somehow by a single stroke. All of the men applauded and shook our hands. Oh, all except one of them. TroubleMan did not join us for the 19th hole.

I decided that day that playing golf provided no outlet for taking charge, unless I intended to become a rules official and be taken seriously when I wrinkled my nose and shook my head. The game did, however, teach me that I am not in charge of results.

Payne Stewart was leading the U.S. Open when his perfect shot down the fairway stopped in a divot full of sand. I can make the most perfect shot, and the ball will hit a sprinkler head and take off like a superball into a bunker.

Lee Janzen's wayward tee shot went into a tree and snuggled there awhile before it fell out and he won the U.S. Open. I can make the worst shot, and the ball will roll, roll, roll right into the hole.

The results are beyond my control. All I can do is try to the best of my ability — ability that, I think it's best for even my instructors to accept, has limitations. I started playing golf at 35, when my knees were already well worn from too many aerobics classes in my 20s, and I have always chosen an engrossing book over a good walk.

Marc and I got along so well for so many years because we accepted each other's limitations and appreciated each other's efforts. When that started to change, I cannot pinpoint. I do remember the day I realized we had a problem.

CHAPTER TEN

In The Hazard

In the Waveside Room at the Bodega Harbour Lodge, guests filled the lines of a creamy white album with advice, congratulations, and wishes — lots of it referencing pars, birdies, OB, and golf in general. My brother Carl, married at the time, served up this metaphor: "Remember, the bunker shot is just as important as the drive to the open fairway. Sometimes you just have to taste some sand to get what you want and get things to work out."

One night in our first year in our house, Marc came home from the golf course hammered after too many vodkas at the 19th hole. I knew better to argue with a drunk, but he had gotten behind the wheel and driven home in that condition and I could not be silent. (His defense: we lived so close, what could go wrong?) In the ensuing argument, he gave me what was to him a playful shove, and I lost my feet and fell backward onto the bed. I quickly got up, packed a suitcase, and checked into a hotel across town for the night.

When I came home the next evening from work and we talked, he tried to joke about what had happened. I looked him firmly in the eye and said, "No. We were having an argument and you pushed me. If you want to argue about who is bigger and stronger, you win, I concede. But let me tell you, if you ever again so much as touch me in anger, I am out of here and this marriage is over. Got it?"

He grew very serious, and nodded. He knew I meant it. And though he did not apologize, he never again came close to me during a conflict.

Our conflicts started to have a theme. On top of his primary vice, pot, Marc did not seem to have any self-control when it came to drinking. He could not have one or two. And he could not refrain from driving even when he'd had three or four.

At first when we would go out to dinner or to a party, I would figure he would drive because he was bigger and it would take him longer to reach the legal limit. But after I started to notice that he didn't seem to pay any attention to that, I would ask ahead of time, which one of us is drinking and which one of us is driving. It seemed like an adult conversation to have, and I certainly did not expect Marc to have to do all the driving just because he was the man. But then I began to notice that even when it was agreed that I was drinking and he was driving, he was still drinking. So I could choose between monitoring him and then nagging when he was having too many, or just saying the hell with it and figuring I would be driving us home if I wanted to make sure we were safe. The worst-case scenario would be for him to agree to be the driver and go over the limit while I did too, then neither of us should be driving home. If that were the case, I'd want to call a cab and Marc would want the keys.

We did not seem to be able to talk about this, or other important matters, rationally. I was working mostly days, and by the time I got home most nights, Marc was already on his way to a medicated state where caring communication was impossible. His long weekends of work, starting with a long drive somewhere before the sun came up Friday morning, brought him home in such a miserable state that my wifely duty was to give him plenty of space each evening so he could smoke, have a few drinks, and play darts in the garage with our buddy from next door.

So even as Marc went back to work for his best man in 2005 and our finances stabilized, our relationship became mired in sand we could not taste. I couldn't see what was wrong, but I didn't think he was happy and I started to suggest that we needed some help.

"I have good health insurance and there's an employee assistance program, why don't we talk to someone?"

He would greet this suggestion with scorn, insinuating that I wouldn't like what I would hear if we did that.

"And suppose you are told to do something that you don't want to do?" he asked.

So clueless by now about what was happening, I did not know why he was asking me this or what he wanted me to say. I knew there was no one more important to me than Marc, nothing more important to me than our marriage, and I was more afraid to do nothing than to do something.

One Thursday in the spring of 2006, I was working at home in my office on a complicated *Home&Garden* story that was due the next day. *Home&Garden* had me back up to full-time again in a job that challenged me on a team that energized me, but it had been a rough week at home with Marc, who had more frequently been coming home bouncing off walls. The night before, I had slept in the guest room because he had passed out snoring loudly.

Now he was down the street playing golf. He had joined a club that played at first light on Tuesdays and Thursdays, a group of gentlemen who were such pleasant company that even at that chilly hour I sometimes joined in, coffee warming my hands. Marc often stayed at the course and played another 18 because he had a monthly card that allowed unlimited golf on weekdays. But on this day at lunchtime, he got a ride back to the house to tell me someone had taken the keys to his truck. He was high and drunk and agitated, and he got on the phone to call his supervisor, who was by now a friend of ours, and tell her he wasn't sure he'd be able to work the next day because he didn't know if he'd have his truck to drive.

"Oh, you'll be working," I told him. "Even if you have to rent a truck."

He left shortly and I took a deep breath to refocus on my work — but not before I made a call-back to say, "Don't worry, he'll be there tomorrow. He's just having a little too much fun today."

And before I took one more step on that ena-bler/codependent wheel, I emailed a good friend whose partner had undergone drug and alcohol rehab in a 30-day inpatient program a year or two before. I told her what had been going on, and that I was thinking it might be a good idea for me to leave for a while, except that it was my house too and I didn't really have anywhere to go.

"Oh, I had the feeling things were not quite right at home," she replied. "Of course, he needs help, and you need to get out of there." I could stay with this cousin of hers or that one, and I could get my butt to Al-Anon for family-friend counseling even if he didn't want to get any help.

Marc got his keys back that day but not his sobriety, so I steered clear that night and did not discuss things or sleep with him. For all I knew, a well-meaning friend had seen the state he was in and confiscated his keys. He left early the next morning for the weekend job, and I called late in the morning.

"Listen, I know you were without your house keys much of the day and now you're gone for the weekend," I said. "I don't know where they were, so I just want to know if you think maybe I should have the locks changed since I am in the house by myself."

He at least gave me the consideration of seeming to think about this for a moment before saying no, he thought I would be okay. I said, this cannot go on and we will talk about the rest when you get home.

After filing that *Home&Garden* story, I spent much of my weekend researching alcoholism and marijuana abuse and learning about my role in Marc's relationship with his vices. The first point was that if it was creating problems in our marriage, then Marc had a problem. The next: I had to stop accepting this behavior and start holding Marc accountable. And of course the hardest, bleakest fact: no one could help him unless he wanted to be helped.

The experts insisted that he would not want to be helped until he had hit rock bottom.

But what is rock bottom for one partner in a marriage without identical consequences for the other? I was unwilling to share the guilt if Marc were to hurt or kill someone because he was driving under the influence, and I did not want to lose my house and savings to pay for a trial or restitution in case he was sued or committed some crime. In California, one partner in a marriage cannot go to rock bottom financially without taking the other along.

It didn't occur to me to tell him I wanted him to leave until he got cleaned up. I couldn't think of anyone else to talk to him — our friends were mostly mine, our relatives mostly distant, and those closest to him were the people who drank and smoked pot with him.

So on Monday, my one-woman intervention began with a plea for him to get some help. He took me seriously, but decided that rather than go to rehab or AA — where surely all of his substance issues would be addressed — he would just stop drinking. We subsequently went on our least expensive golf vacation ever, because I decided that if he wasn't going to drink, I wouldn't either. Not a glass of wine was sipped, and all of the friends looking forward to opening a special bottle could not use us as an excuse.

Of course I now understand this exercise was pointless. To stop drinking while continuing to smoke pot and refusing to address the underlying problem saves money but solves nothing. On that trip, his misery emerged behind the wheel. Twice he was stopped, once on the way for speeding and, on the way home, for aggressive driving and tailgating in traffic. The first officer accepted his excuse that he had just passed someone and hadn't quite slowed down sufficiently, issuing just a warning. The second saw Marc's frustration and exasperation with the way everyone else was driving, and asked him to please, just calm down behind the wheel. I sat in the passenger's seat wishing the highway patrolman would hear what my mind was saying: "Please, please, give him a ticket. He is getting out of control." But he didn't hear. He just gave us both a sad look.

I insisted we needed couples counseling, and Marc refused. I suggested he have counseling on his own, and he refused.

So I decided to have my own couples counseling. I went to my health provider and filled out a bunch of forms and had my first meeting with a therapist.

"Your problem is very clear," she told me. "Your husband is a substance abuser, and you are co-dependent. And until you address that, you cannot get at any other problems you may have in your relationship."

She directed me to a family-and-friends group that met weekly, and agreed to meet weekly with me as well for as long as my plan allowed. She also put me on the waiting list for a "boundaries" group for women that she seemed to think essential for me to learn to draw lines in the sand.

"Otherwise, other than some anxiety that you can treat with meditation and exercise, there is nothing wrong with you."

My anxiety was about to have a reprieve. That fall, I made my first trip to the High Point Furniture Market in North Carolina, stopping first for a few lively days with my friend Kristin in New York. As I chatted with New York cabbies and bonded with home and garden journalists, I realized how comfortable I felt with myself again. I wasn't going to my room at night wondering what shape my roommate would be in, or worrying about what I might or might not say that would set him off somehow. I became more determined than ever not to accept the way things were. They simply weren't acceptable and I did not want to go back to being the cautious, guarded Susan I had become at home, I wanted to be the friendly, funny, and unselfconscious person I had become again on this journey. I was going to improve my marriage. Or, I thought in the back of my mind, end it. But, no, Marc and I together would make it better than ever.

When I was about to come home, Marc talked about the weekend ahead, and I said, "But where are you working?" He dusted me off, saying he'd tell me about that later. I had an odd feeling.

I had not been home long when Marc told me his best man had fired him over an in-store incident, so unjustly it seemed from what he told me. I gave him a big hug and told him I was so sorry that happened, and he said, "This is just what I was hoping for."

We went to see one of my paralegal school teachers to see if he had any recourse, and she wrote a letter on his behalf. I came to learn that the reason for the firing had less to do with the incident — where a customer said she felt intimidated when he warned her forcefully that her proximity to the food samples was creating a health violation — than with Marc's disinclination to stand up and take responsibility and make amends for what had happened. On the phone with his boss, he justified his actions instead of apologizing for them, and then said he had to go because he was running late for his tee time.

I began to feel I was living with a time bomb.

My personal therapist yelled at me for not reading Marc the riot act now. But in just two months, my parents were celebrating their 50th anniversary, and I did not want to give them any of this news. I wanted to go to Baltimore and have a nice time — which, oddly, Marc and I continued to do together even through it all — and then get serious about the work that had to be done with my husband.

***

One day during our visit to Charm City, Marc fainted in front of my father, who did his best to keep the big guy from going down and doing any serious damage. A statue got knocked off its pedestal, but Marc did not strike any hard surface. I remembered that a few years earlier, he had fainted at the golf course and met a shoe cleaner with his nose, requiring stitches. I thought maybe that was pot-induced, but this time Marc was traveling without his weed. When I got sick the next day, we figured it was just something going around.

Marc and I had a wonderful time otherwise. He had long talks with cousins I hardly knew, and made a point of occupying the kids at the party. We watched the New Year's Eve fireworks at the Inner Harbor and spent a couple of nights in a nice hotel, where Marc nursed me when I was sick.

And a few days after we came home, I said, okay, this is it: I have been going to counseling, and what I am hearing is that you are a substance abuser and I am co-dependent. So if you want to stay married, either you are going to have counseling on your own or we are going to have to see if we can find someone who will give us couples counseling.

Marc was furious, as he finally saw this as an ultimatum, not in so many words. We got on the phone with my employee assistance program to get some free couples counseling sessions lined up, and then crashed and burned at our very first meeting with a doctor who pointed out to Marc that the pot he was smoking was not as harmless as the pot we had all smoked in our youth, that it was many times stronger and more mind-altering. He challenged Marc's relationship with the weed, and Marc said, this is not going to work.

We left quietly, and in the car on the way home, I said we would make our separation as amicable and respectful as possible.

Marc nodded but said, "Why don't we try someone else?"

"Fine, why don't you pick out someone? Maybe a woman would be a better choice for us."

He found not just a woman, but a woman with expertise in art therapy AND couples counseling AND substance issues. They talked on the phone and she said she would require him not to smoke pot or drink on the day of our session, and he agreed. And on the ferry taking me to work the morning of our first session, I took out a notebook and began writing the ways that Marc's pot use and drinking were hurting our marriage.

I quickly had 10 stark, brutal statements ranging from things like, "I feel completely responsible for our finances because Marc won't pursue a job that does drug-testing," to "I lose sleep when Marc comes home late crashing into furniture," to "We can't talk about our problems because Marc can't stay in the discussion and starts repeating himself and then says that I'm not listening to him," to "Marc escapes problems instead of addressing and solving them, and so there are fewer and fewer friends and family members in our lives."

I read them out loud and Angela asked Marc if any of these things sounded like problems for him. He shrugged and said no, not really. The only problem that he had, he said, was that his wife thought he had a problem. I gave him a copy of my list, though, and his family found it still among his things when he died. This, and other notes I wrote pleading for him to get help so that we could spend the rest of our lives together the way we'd promised. Was there something he'd like me to do in the meantime, I asked him? Lose 10 pounds maybe? Work on some issue of my own? Dye my hair red? Please just tell me.

But there didn't seem to be. After only a few sessions, with Angela guiding us to reminders of how much we loved each other, we could agree that we wanted to try to work things out. We started talking about things differently, and when we looked at our finances and the value of our house, we pretty easily agreed to put it on the market and rent an even better house, even closer to the golf course, for even less than our monthly housing costs. With the profit banked, Marc could freely pursue a new career in remodeling and construction without me worrying about how the bills would be paid or feeling we had to sacrifice golf vacations that I had worked all year to earn.

Angela brimmed with positive reinforcement. Later she said she always saw the love, there was no question about that. The question was, would Marc do what still needed to be done?

CHAPTER ELEVEN

Out Of Bound(arie)s

P ia Nilsson and Lynn Marriott, a couple of women who teach golf in Arizona, wrote a book and created a program that's propagated an entire school of thought among golfers. They call it Vision54 — which is based on the goal of a birdie on each hole. On the typical par-72 championship golf course, that's a final score of 54. Annika Sorenstam so idealized the number, she had it embroidered on one of the head covers she carried.

It's not a score that's ever been recorded in an official professional tournament — the best on record so far: 58 by a fortunate few. But, so what, why limit our potential? There is always room for improvement in golf, life, love, all those big little words. The question always is, what are we willing to do to shoot 54? How much *could* we do? How much would we sacrifice? What is it worth to us?

I didn't think I could shoot 54 in marriage, but I would commit time and money that I would never spend on golf to the matrimonial equivalents of training, practicing, and coaching. We were worth that much. The question remained, how much could we do?

We could certainly learn a thing or two. I knew enough about Marc and his past to believe he had problems that went much deeper than our marriage. He had sedated himself since he was 15, and now, especially when he drank too, anger and frustration surfaced. As I read the experts' descriptions about what had happened to me, the co-dependent, during our relationship, I learned about detaching. I needed to separate my inner self from his mess and accept that only he could save himself. I also had to protect my savings and home. That did not mean I had to physically leave: in the friends-and-family support group, I heard many a parent and significant other struggling with how to protect themselves, their assets, and children while still loving the troubled soul in their lives. A middle-aged mother talked about a recent lunch with her daughter, where she noticed how quickly her once-pretty little girl was aging through addiction. "I know I can't give her any more money or have her live with me," she said. "But still, it made me sad." There was no universal formula, and what I concluded was that I would just know when enough was enough.

Detaching had its challenges for me. During this time we went on a fam trip to Alisal, a golf resort outside the town of Solvang down along the central coast of California, for a couples tournament that drew the same guests year after year. The guests were aging now, and the resort hoped a story might attract new money. Yet, it still had some old-school quirks, which I pointed out to Marc a few days before we were to go.

"It says on here that men are expected to wear a jacket to dinner," I noted, handing him the itinerary. I thought about reminding him again, but I let the thought pass because I considered it co-dependent, not to mention nagging.

The first evening, after a practice round of golf, we met the participants at a cocktail party. They were old money, admirers of George W. Bush, and quite outspoken about the liberal commie Democrats of San Francisco. I engaged with them anyway, but Marc had his own old-school quirks and preferred to keep the conversation polite and not political.

Before dinner the next evening, he showered and dressed first because he was going to go get us a glass of wine that we could have in our luxurious cabin. Out he came, every hair in place, smelling great, wearing a nice shirt, a pair of shorts, and sneakers.

"Where's your jacket? Your slacks?" I asked, furious. "You can't go to dinner here like that."

I think he realized right away that he had forgotten the dress code, but he called the restaurant anyway to confirm. "We have a closet full of jackets," Marc was told. "But you've got to wear slacks."

Detach. "I am sorry, but I have to go to the dinner," I said. "They've paid for our trip. If I have to go without you, I will have to go without you."

It was almost 5 on Sunday. He grabbed the keys and left.

And by the time I finished showering and dressing, he rushed in with a couple of bags containing a pair of khakis and a nice-looking pair of slip-on shoes.

"How did you do that?" I asked, stunned at this feat of shopping savvy.

"The stores were all closing. So I knocked on the window of this one, and I think the saleslady felt sorry for me and she let me in."

It was an awkward evening for us. Our host kindly told Marc how he had lived in jackets out of that closet during his first weeks at the resort, and other guests agreed that business might be better served without such restriction, particularly considering the resort's name, Alisal Guest Ranch.

I did not much care for suffering such consequences of detaching, but steeled myself. My close friends seemed to agree with my vague plan. "Yes," they said, "you will know. You are smart, you are strong, you will figure it out. And we are here for you." One night early in our year of counseling, I went to an A's game at the Coliseum with a few of those treasured girlfriends. I had for several years instigated an occasional ritual we called Chickee Night, and sometimes we had as many as 16 in the stands, usually just women but sometimes we'd bestow honorary chickeehood on some men for the evening. I had to leave town suddenly once and miss a Chickee Night because of a death in my family, and Marc, who had to stay behind and work, offered to fill in for me.

The chickees in attendance told me he was an excellent host.

On this night, I had a couple of drinks at the ballpark and took a cab home from the BART station, walking the last block or so. A police car passed me on my quiet street, and I gave a friendly wave. When I arrived at my garage, our usual point of entry, the police car was there in front of it. I slipped around Smokey and let myself in. Marc's truck, I noticed, was still warm and ticking; he must have just come home from the golf course.

Inside the house, I heard water running upstairs and the doorbell ringing out front. There were the two officers outside.

Oh no, I thought, what's going on next door now? It was always something in that house with teenagers.

The police were looking for my husband. I said I had just gotten home from a girls night out — they had seen me, I pointed out — and wasn't sure where he was.

They told me there had been an incident involving a truck that was registered to Marc, that he had tailgated another driver and then when the other driver stopped, Marc spit on him.

"Oh, no, Marc would never do something like that," I protested, even believing myself at first as I thought of the sweet, gentle man I had married. They seemed caught off guard, and they gave me a card with their phone number and told me to have him call them right away. If he didn't, they said, they'd be back.

After they left, Marc came out of the shower giggly and

nonsensical. There was no way I was telling him what had just happened — he might get belligerent or even call the police and they would know the driver of that truck had been drunk. I closed the bedroom door as he passed out, and I turned off the doorbell just in case the police returned during the night. I left their card on our game table with a note saying matter-of-factly that the police had come looking for him and why. "I told them that my husband would never do something like that," I wrote.

We hardly spoke the next day. He had to deal with consequences: he left a message for the police, and when they called back and he quietly began taking responsibility for his actions, I stepped out of the room. I assume he also apologized to the other driver at some point — he never told me how it had all shaken out except to say, when we were looking at rental houses later, that one neighborhood probably was not a good idea because that driver lived there.

Meanwhile, I had my own consequences. My mind was blown. The police, at my house, looking for my husband! That just was not supposed to happen! What was next? Marc was spiraling down, and I was not going to go with him. He obviously needed to deal with his drug and alcohol dependency for me to ever again feel safe in our marriage.

I am pretty sure I stayed with friends that night, and then the next afternoon we met with Angela. Our sweet, positive therapist turned bad cop.

"Do you want to lose your marriage?" she scolded him. "Because that is what is going to happen here."

Marc was so full of remorse, it was hard to berate him. In fact, Angela told us that it is not uncommon for someone doing deep inner work to have a setback like this, but at the same time that she was asking me to hang in there a little longer, she was warning him that his wife was not going to put up with this sort of thing.

And in my boundary therapy group of about eight women with various life predicaments — not all substance related and some of unimaginable horror — one of the practitioners singled me out for homework that week.

"You're going to go home and tell your husband the marriage is over and you want a divorce," she said, using a word I would never speak. "Can you do that?"

I dumbly nodded, yet as soon as I walked out the door I thought, "I'm not doing that. It's not time yet."

The practitioner had overstepped my boundaries, and I returned to the group the following week to say so. Not speaking until I was called on, I was asked if I had done my homework.

"No."

Had I left the room thinking I would?

"No."

But then why had I said I would?

I didn't have a good answer but one of my fellow groupies did. She observed that the practitioner had authority and was there to help us, and so the first instinct would be to do what she said. But it was obviously not at all what I wanted to do.

I was not going to stay in my marriage unless my husband got help, I said. But I had no friends and family nearby to call on to have an intervention. We were in counseling with a therapist he trusted. I needed to take this time to give Marc a chance, as much as I could, to help himself.

Yes, it was hard, almost unbearable, to live from day to day not knowing what the future held, to be having various therapy appointments every single week, to be in this place where I did not know if I would soon be single again or might instead have a true partner. But fear of that future was not driving me. I was making an informed choice. I had taken vows, made an eternal commitment, and if it took a few months or a year out of my life to go to counseling with Marc and give him a look at that chance, I could do it. If I had any fear, it was of the regret I would always have if I did not do it.

"Do you want to stay in the group?" I was asked.

"I don't think so," I said. "Tonight I walked in on a beautiful spring evening thinking of all the other things I could be doing instead — working in the garden, hitting balls at the range, going to a ballgame, cooking a nice dinner. I'll let you know."

The next day I called and dropped out. I don't know if the facilitator had made a mistake or accomplished her mission, if I had passed or if I had failed. Was the answer to Marc's question "What will you do if they tell you to do something you don't want to do?" then "Whatever I want to do"?

I don't think it was that simple. If the practitioner had said in front of us both, "Susan, if you really want to help Marc, you have to leave him," that would have been different. Instead, she seemed to be making a decision about what I needed, and I could do that myself.

So I went home to life as usual, a pretty simple and joyful life, fixing us dinners and making tee times and letting Marc know how much I loved him. In my way, I thought I was reminding him how high the stakes were and why it was we were going out of our way every Friday for an hour of counseling that often made us uncomfortable. Instead of letting him fall to rock bottom, I thought, why don't I show him what he'll be missing if he doesn't straighten himself out?

Not that I put it in those terms. I never did give Marc an ultimatum, not even at the end.

Angela said I hardened after a visit by my parents that August. Marc was supposed to work that week, but there was no work and I guess he took it out on all of us instead of finding something else to keep himself busy. He was irritable and rude to me and to my parents, and as soon as they left we went on vacation to our favorite destination. I kicked his butt ferociously to win the Plumas Cup running away. I slept in my own room. I cried a lot and did not talk to him much. It was my vacation, I had worked for it, I wasn't going to let him ruin it. Ha.

Marc seemed oblivious to my pain, however. So when we came home I asked him what he was going to do to make things right with my parents. He never made things right, seeing the issue as me picking my parents over him, and in some way I was finished. But we kept going to counseling, which began to turn sharply toward Marc's substance issues — subtly at first, and then a two-woman intervention. (Angela called it a one-woman intervention but her leadership motivated me.) One night in mid-January, Marc hadn't come home or called by dark — so unusual for him that at around nine I made a call or two. Then I heard the garage open and the truck backing in. Marc opened his door and fell out, came in the house giggling, and went upstairs.

Detach, I told myself in my corner of the couch. Breathe. Then I heard a crash upstairs. Detach...uh, wait, he could be hurt. As I moved toward the stairs, I was relieved to hear giggling.

That night I slept in the second bedroom, and the next day I told Marc that I would not be sharing a bed with him again until he cleaned up. "You can take a little time to figure out what you're going to do," I said, as I began moving more and more things into the other room.

Still, we did things together and made dates. For my 50th birthday, we headed to Carmel Valley to watch the Super Bowl and play golf and taste wine, and as we sat together canoodling in the golf cart on the last day, Marc said, "See how things can be if we're just nice to each other?"

About a week later I headed east for a relative's 100th

birthday celebration. Marc was not working much and we could not justify spending money for him to go, but I did not want him to anyway. Before I left, I wrote him a letter and assembled a file full of information on rehab and recovery programs. I told him whatever he wanted to do, whatever it cost, we would do it.

Marc never said a word to me about that file. When I came home, we hugged. "Did you miss me?" he asked. "Of course. I always miss you," I said, with a lump in my throat, thinking, hoping, maybe now he was going to tell me his plan. He smiled, maybe seeing the hope on my face, and gave me a kiss. I'll never forget the bewildered look on his face as I then went to what was now my room.

There was a moment in counseling when he saw it all. By now, Angela was telling him he needed to come in for individual therapy, and I was telling him he needed to get treatment for the pot and alcohol. Every argument or plea was fair game in the desperation of the time. "Look, you love the movies," I said one day as we sat side by side on one of Angela's deep couches. "In every movie, there's this scene where the hero, the protagonist, gets to decide something or say something or do something that changes everything. It's the big scene, the one it's all about. This is your big scene, Marc. This is your chance to change the way all of this has been going and make a fresh start."

As I tried to summon my next great argument, I was watching his face. And to my surprise, he looked at me and there was this flicker, this recognition, this understanding I had not seen and by now did not expect to see. He actually appeared to be considering how this scene might play out.

It shocked me. I held my breath, waiting for him to say... OH, OKAY, I'M IN?... I'M READY?... I don't know what exactly. The lines were not in my mind's script.

But just that quickly, a curtain dropped over those beautiful eyes. I think at that moment, he weighed me and our life together against his life with pot and alcohol, and he made a choice he would never be able to unmake.

If I could have one mulligan in our life together, this would be it: I would, in that moment when he saw me so clearly, get down on my knees and beg him to please, *please* do what we were asking him to do, do it for us, do it for me, because I love you and I don't want to lose you but I cannot keep living like this.

The moment passed so swiftly. And there was never another one like it.

In a short conversation toward the end of February 2008, I told Marc that I accepted that he did not want to stop smoking pot, and I wanted to separate. He nodded sadly and said he would look for a place to live.

That Friday, I went to counseling. He didn't.

CHAPTER TWELVE

Golf With Girls, Finally

The Sharp Park Business Women's Golf Club splashed onto my radar screen when I splashed a couple of shots into the water on the second hole of San Mateo's Poplar Creek Golf Course in the spring of 2007. It was the first round of the San Mateo Women's Golf Championship, an annual fem-fest like no other I knew of in the Bay Area. Gary and Eva Monisteri ran the golf course at the time — well, big Gary ran it, but as he will readily admit, his blonde, Swedish wife wore the family golf crown. Oh, she was just such a fine player. Slender in stature but big on grit, she had played for the San Jose State team that won the NCAA championship, and now helped Gary run the shop at the course. (Eva was the first pro shop buyer to tell me that women would rather not have logos on their shirts and jackets because we want our clothes to multi-task, the way that we do.) Later, after giving birth to a daughter and a son, she

129

would win the San Francisco City Championship and twice qualify for U.S. Mid-Amateurs. Marc and I treasured our rounds of golf with this amiable couple.

It was Eva who started and operated the women's championship, a two-day tournament open to women of all levels of both golf and income. You didn't have to belong to a particular club to play, and Eva kept the entry fee under $50 by hitting up all of her suppliers for tee prizes and awards. The good players competed on equal ground for the championship trophy, and the rest of us were grouped by handicap to compete in flights where we subtracted our allotted strokes for our official score. At the end of it all, we'd watch the groups coming into the clubhouse trying to avoid the pond just right of the hill-and-dale 18th green, then sit down for lunch and a festive awards celebration.

The first year I played, I won my flight with the lowest scores I had ever shot, even though I had had to call a penalty on myself when one of my fellow competitors asked me to move my ball marker for her putt and I failed to return it for my putt. Yes, I know nobody was home watching on TV, but when we golfers break a rule we are supposed to penalize ourselves. It can be a problem that so few of us know all of the rules. Golf honchos like to say, well, there are only 34 rules. However, *The Rules of Golf* is 97 pages long and there's an explanatory companion book called *Decisions on the Rules of Golf* that is another 400-and-some pages. (I believe the latter volume gets longer with every new edition.)

To really understand it all, you need a third book, *The*

Rules of Golf in Plain English, another 142 pages written by a couple of — oh happy joy joy — lawyers, and a fourth book that has yet to be written, *Exactly How to Play Golf by the Damned Rules.* There are irritating women known as rules divas, or, worse, rules nazis, who will tell us what we ought to be doing whether or not they really know what they are talking about. Very few people can truly understand and explain the rules of golf — and of this I am sure because I have had the pleasure of knowing one or two of those few. They aren't the ones telling us what we ought to be doing, unless we ask them.

I have all the bossiness required of a rules nazi; however, I know how little I really know. Instead, I'm one of those irritating women who will tell everyone what is wrong with the rules and how they ought to be changed. For instance, the rule I broke is as backward as the hole-in-one ritual that demands the lucky one buy everyone else drinks in the bar after the round. No kidding? I'd just done my competition a kindness by moving my marker out of her putting line so that her golf ball wouldn't hit it and roll astray, yet she was under no obligation to remind me to move my marker back and the penalty strokes were all mine even though the whole thing was her idea. Harrumph!

Now this day when I took an 11 on Poplar Creek's par-4 second hole would serve up yet another reminder of how little I know about the rules, and also teach me a lesson in grace. Because after my 11, I remarked to my companions that maybe a breakfast beer was in order to settle my nerves, and they hailed the cart girl even though it was three hours before noon. Now we were friends.

Cheryl M. and Ann, a bit older than me and not your stereotypical country club ladies, golfed between cigarettes as they cruised the short and very walkable course in their cart. (An extreme example of a country club lady: I played with a woman at the ultra-luxe Grand Del Mar resort in San Diego who kept coming to the green without her putter. I finally teased her about this, and she replied apologetically, "When I play at my club, my caddie brings my putter to the green.")

I learned that Ann waitressed at a famous old hotel restaurant in San Francisco, and Cheryl M. was a loan officer for one of the banks that, we didn't know then, wouldn't survive the economic crisis to come. There was no talking about husbands, kids or dogs — we were all golf. And when we got to the 16th hole and Ann hit her ball left of the tree line and outside the white boundary stakes, we referred to the day's rule sheet, which stated that the "out of bounds left of the 16th fairway is in play."

I rationalized that the mere presence of this statement on our sheet meant that Ann could go play her ball. After all, if we were playing by the rules of golf, the white stakes would be statement enough that the ball was out of play, right? Our rule sheet wouldn't have to tell us that.

I must have sounded like I knew what I was talking about, because Ann and Cheryl M. discussed it, but ultimately shrugged. Ann did not re-tee to hit her third shot, the way she would if she had hit her tee shot out of bounds. Instead, she drove into the neighboring fairway to smack the first ball through the trees and back into our fairway.

Wouldn't you know, she was spotted over there by one of the "rules nazi" types, who scolded her and said she was out of bounds.

Ann finished the hole, but after the round the rules nazi reported her to the Monisteris and she was disqualified from the tournament. I looked over at her in embarrassment, but she kindly shook her head at me and said, "It wasn't your fault, and I wasn't in it anyway." And she returned the next day to play the second round despite her disqualification. Pretty well, too, as I recall.

I joined Ann and Cheryl M. at their lunch table and saw familiar faces I had enjoyed playing with in the past at the San Mateo Women's Championship. Nora... Stephanie... Lauren... All of them were members of the Sharp Park Business Women's Golf Club. Most of them walked, played fast, and didn't have their husbands or fathers or sons coming along to caddie and get in the way of the rest of us. Several members are gay, and so one year the club had a "Which Way Do You Swing?" tournament. They played by the rules, posted their scores, and were, true to their name, all business on the course but having a lot of fun, the way I wanted to be.

And so darned nice. Cheryl M., a fellow golf slut, befriended me that year and invited me to play in her other club's invitational that August. I am not sure whether she thought I would help her team or whether I would just be game enough to dress up in the ridiculous outfit she concocted each year to fit the unique theme. One year we wore kimonos and wigs (adorned with chopsticks) for the Asia-and-the-Pacific theme. Another year we looked like waiters in berets, armed with baguettes and wine bottles, for the Parisian mode (for once, no wig!). Best of all, we chose Jamaica in the international pot luck and came in Rastafarian wigs, wearing sunglasses and T-shirts and "smoking" joints.

We won as geishas and didn't play very well as Jamaicans though we found the in-cart reggae beat soothing to our swings.

Cheryl M., a divorced mom with two great grown kids, knew how to have a good time, and she did. She loved to cook a rich cream sauce and serve it over pasta with a luscious Chardonnay. Her golf swing forced many an eye to avert, because she'd somehow whirl the club around her girth and loop it, a la Jim Furyk, to hit the ball square. Yet she broke 90 at Sharp Park once — no simple achievement on such a raggedy course — and generally broke 100, riding along in her cart with the Sunday paper's puzzles in hand. She hated to decline any invitation to play golf. Even on Mother's Day, she'd tell the kids and her own mother, we can have dinner together *after* my round, not instead of it.

Once or twice, she brought me out to Sharp Park on a Sunday as her guest, and when the club that had kept my handicap, the California Golf Writers Association, decided to drop its USGA golf affiliation, I shifted over to Sharp Park beginning in 2008, the year Marc and I agreed to separate. Originally I figured I would just play a few rounds there, but that spring I suddenly needed something to do, someplace to be, on my favorite day of the week. This 31-and-a-half-mile drive took me out of my hollow home and into another world. In Alameda, the fog would be burning off as I left and the sun might be shining through the Bay Bridge, but as I passed through San Francisco, climbed to the coast and then dropped down into Pacifica, the fog could be hanging over the course and the temperature might have dropped 12 degrees. In Pacifica, I played a long, shaggy municipal course instead of Alameda's short, well-groomed city courses.

And I left behind my husband and spent the day with 10 to 20 women who didn't ask me about him. I remembered this gratefully years later, when a woman I was interviewing told me that she didn't feel she fit in with the first golf club she joined because nobody asked her about her family. She had just lost a son, and she wanted to share but this group seemed cold to her. My group seemed generous to me for not asking. They were my escape from the saddest time in my life, when I was sleeping across the hall from the man I had promised to love for the rest of my life, knowing we weren't going to spend the rest of our lives together, waiting for him to move out as we had agreed he would.

The house was so quiet and empty with the two of us there living separately. Marc wasn't working full-time that spring, and of course he still smoked, so even great credit and ample savings weren't getting him accepted into the apartments he liked. Maybe he thought I would change my mind about wanting to separate. Of course I hoped he would change his mind about the pot. Still, it dumbfounded me to hear him say one day, after a few months of this, "I feel like you're just waiting for me to leave." Yes. I was.

Once or twice, I suggested we go out and play golf together. He would either shake his head sadly or look at me in utter disdain.

I stayed with friends as often as I could, and planned outings and getaways to have more significant time out of the house. During one of them, a special annual golf media fam in Tahoe in early June, Marc figured to be moving out.

"I'd like to not be here when you are moving," I said. "So, if you need a few more days, I'll call toward the end and see if I can just stay up there longer."

My first task on the trip was to work on a story for *Home&Garden* on Tahoe interiors, and one of the area's busy designers took me on a tour of her work, which included the expansion of her own charming cabin near Donner Lake. We sat in the sunshine having lunch afterward, and as happens so often with women, the conversation turned personal. She had taken a big inner journey with her husband as they looked at their lives in response to a life-altering event. When I told her my husband and I were separating, and why, and that in fact I expected to return from this trip to an empty house, her face twisted in witness to my pain. Then it lit up and she said so kindly, "What a wonderful, amazing opportunity for you!" She chose to share hope about the opening of a new chapter rather than commiserate over the closing of the old one. I know the tears were slipping below my sunglasses, I was so touched by the caring of a stranger and also so relieved to finally leave my discrete limboland of the previous few months and be able to tell others my truth about what had happened.

I also told our fam tour host, who had become a friend over the years to us both. He said he was sorry and hoped I could relax and have fun over the course of this week in the mountains and along glittering Lake Tahoe, the site of which could awe and inspire the most troubled of souls. Even though we would be playing some of the courses that Marc and I had most loved — including some of our Plumas Cup favorites, like Whitehawk Ranch and the Dragon — the familiarity of the golf and mix of new and old faces comforted me. On the last day of the golf excursion, I participated in a delightful test of the handicap system never experienced before or after: playing in a group of four players of wide-ranging ability, we all stood up on the Dragon's scenic complex of first tees and selected the tees that we thought suited our games. I picked the two-dragon tees up front, a senior player chose the three-dragons right behind me, a pretty good local player took the four-dragons, and our big-hitting host went back to the five-dragons.

Having a foursome play from four different sets of tees can lengthen a round by the time it takes everyone to get in position, but it was a quiet morning so we took our time. When we sat down at the end and adjusted our scores for handicaps and tees, we had all shot around net par! Most important, we all had felt competent, as if we were playing a golf course that had been set up for us to enjoy. I had never really liked that golf course, which had been built with a goal of challenging those who took it on. Its slogan had been "Send Me Your Heroes," which I had simplified to "Screw You." But new ownership, great company and a handicapping experiment made that day memorable.

Marc was still in the house.

I stayed in the mountains another day or two and then really had to come back down the hill. It was the week of the U.S. Open that Marc moved out, taking along our 50-inch plasma TV because I told him he had picked it out, he had set it up, and he had done most of the watching, it was his. In another conversation about who was keeping what, I asked if I could keep a figure of a fierce Indian warrior because, I said, "It might protect me." He could keep the second in the pair, I told him. "But what if their power is only when they are together, and separately they have none?' he asked me. Having lost what we wanted most, we didn't argue about property, except in the "No, you take it," vein. He sweetly set up my new 42-inch television (plenty fine for picking up the flight of the dimpled ball in HD) so that I wouldn't miss Tiger and Phil battle it out at Torrey Pines.

When I moved a year later, I saw that he had attached to all of the wires and cables little slips of paper that identified what connected where, so that I would be able to put it all back together.

Oh, and as it turned out, there would indeed be an epic, unforgettable duel at Torrey Pines that week — between Tiger and Rocco Mediate, not Phil. Tiger limping and Rocco ebullient, the two battled it out right down to a Monday morning playoff that I watched by myself feeling nothing but relief in the quiet all around me.

Indeed, basking in the warm tranquility of the corner of the couch lit by morning sunlight through the clerestory window, my relief embarrassed me. Even after many months of counseling and pleading, a few more of surrender and sorrow, "I'm so glad my husband finally moved out," was not a socially acceptable admission. "I'm so glad my husband finally moved out, but, damn, I had to go buy a new TV," was even worse.

Then a month or so later, there was newlywed Greg Norman leading the British Open on Sunday morning with his new bride, Chris Evert, providing calm commentary behind the ropes. Norman was 53, Evert 54. Norman lost. But that the two of them, second time around, had found each other and were clearly deliriously happy consoled 50-year-old me in my raw aloneness so early on a Sunday morning on the couch I had not lost. Maybe there was hope for me too, I thought. (Or maybe not — Evert and Norman were over after just 15 months.)

I spent the rest of the summer quietly, grieving with a friend who had lost her mother. We were emotionally overwrought, avoiding alcohol and extreme social situations. My best friend, who had also lost her mother, came for a healing visit that included spa time, long walks, and one over-the-top dinner that did include exquisite wine and cost us each $200. On the last day, we toured the Frida Kahlo exhibition at SFMOMA and I stood for a long time in front of the painter's largest work, *The Two Fridas*. The Frida on the left has a heart torn open and bleeding onto her white frock. The Frida on the right's heart is whole. The two hold hands. *The Two Fridas* took a powerful grip on my own heart, because I had often, through many difficult months when I had to be strong through pain, envisioned my strong hand holding my own heartbroken hand. In the most unbearable times, I believe I had literally taken one hand in the other.

One early Monday morning I went out to play golf by myself, and ended up joining a newlywed police officer my age who said, "I've got a lot of friends who would love to meet a lady who plays golf." I was not ready, I told him reluctantly.

I had promised myself I wouldn't rebound dangerously out into the world of men, and there would be no dating in 2008. It was my golf-with-the-girls time, and Sharp Park represented church, spa, cocoon. And lo and behold, there I was at my first Turkey Shoot, getting my first hole-in-one — fittingly, with Cheryl M. as a witness. It was just your straightforward perfect shot with a 9-iron that landed on the green and kept on rolling on our littlest hole, the 91-yard eighth. I didn't believe it, I thought for sure the ball must be hiding just behind the flag, so Cheryl M. drove up to confirm the feat so that she, Margo, Nora, and I could jump up and down screaming and hollering and hugging.

I took my frozen turkey prize home to an empty house and cried.

By November, Marc and I didn't socialize together or even talk much, so it was over the phone that I told him I'd finally had my first hole-in-one. He made me tell him all about it, and was complimentary. But his voice was very soft over the phone, and there was a sadness between us. Through hundreds of rounds of golf together, we had witnessed at least four holes-in-one by companions and a few close calls for each other. Every time we played together, it was a little miracle we might get to share.

Maybe in the next world. One of my golf club friends likes to think of her late husband, her late father, and any of her other golfing loved ones, teeing off whenever they like on heavenly courses. In December of 2012, we learned that Cheryl M. had joined them. Her daughter, Rachael, found her sitting in her favorite chair by the fire, a glass of wine by her side. She was only 63 but had had heart surgery that summer. Rachael came to our golf club Christmas party a few days later with her brother, Ethan, and told us that although she herself was too hyperactive for the game, she understood her mother's love for it. "Mom always said you could learn everything you needed to know about a person by playing a round of golf with them," Rachael said. "It was the source of so much enjoyment for her."

Of course we all had the opportunity to say something about Cheryl M. that day. I looked around at all the sad faces and couldn't collect myself enough to tell them that it was Cheryl M. who had brought me to this group of friends and I would always be grateful to her for that. But I did tell her family that I had gotten onto the freeway that morning thinking sadly of how much I'd miss her, and then I saw a rainbow.

CHAPTER THIRTEEN

Golf With Guys, Again

I chilled a special bottle of bubbly from Mumm Napa Valley and planned an introspective New Year's Eve on my couch to ring in 2009.

Yet when I opened a notebook to write whatever came to mind, whatever came to mind amounted to one big "Fuck you 2008 and good riddance." Not many words flowed. Maybe I was done with introspection.

I'd done so much of that, with and without help. When I showed Angela my brand new "gottagogolf" Match.com profile a few days later, she practically applauded said, "I really thought you were ready after your trip in the fall."

That trip was a budget-blowing three weeks on the East Coast that began in late September in a place I'd long wanted to visit, Charleston, South Carolina, and ended in New York City. First I ate my way around the city full of gardens, history, and Southern charm for a few days, staying at the

Vendue Inn, where the manager made her way from guest to guest at breakfast each morning and greeted me warmly by name when I ran into her on the street in her own neighborhood.

I felt myself emerging again. I was talking to strangers and taking an interest in my surroundings and coming back to life. I unselfconsciously sampled five-star menus at the restaurants' bars, accidentally discovering the most delightful way for a single person to dine with fascinating company. Exploring the historic streets, I popped into bars with TV screens to watch some of the Ryder Cup, the semi-annual team matches between the best male golfers of the United States and Europe, and ended up telling my seat mates about my golf-writing experience. And on Ryder Cup Sunday, I headed out for a few days' stay on Kiawah Island, where *The Legend of Bagger Vance* had been filmed.

The island mixes protected marshland and wildlife in among swanky houses and the Sanctuary, a resort for the rich. Its golf courses mostly weave in and out of all of the above, and I got out of the car to play what I was told was the ladies' choice, Osprey Point.

The starter sent me out on the course all by myself, but not before warning me about the alligators. My reality check came on the 10th tee, when I stepped up to hit my drive alongside some small alligator statues. I whacked the ball and one nodded at me.

This first round of golf of this special vacation brought out the best in my game, and I almost broke 90. The friendly starter — and by now I was thinking "friendly" to be redundant as a description for anybody in the Charleston region, from drug store clerk to five-star restaurant server — saw me finishing early, and he told me about his own post-divorce trip up north years earlier. He tried dishes he'd never eaten, he said, because he'd vowed not to say no to any offers of meals. I took this to heart — not that I was one to decline any offers of meals in the first place, but as a golf slut I liked the "say yes" metaphor. "Where should I go to watch the Ryder Cup?" I asked him. He said he thought the sensible place to go would be the Ryder Cup Bar in the clubhouse at the Ocean Course.

Well, of course! I got directions and found my way to the site of the 1991 Ryder Cup, where all of the TVs were tuned in for what only that morning had seemed sure to be another U.S. loss. By the time I arrived and took in the ocean view outside, the unlikely heroes who were drawing eyes to a riveting scene in Louisville, Kentucky, included Boo Weekly, Anthony Kim, Kenny Perry, and captain Paul Azinger. We won while I put away a bowl of she crab soup.

My fam host at Kiawah had arranged my golf in the proper order, with Osprey followed by Cougar Point and then finally on the last day the Ocean Course. It is the Ocean Course that even now I sometimes dream about.

It is first of all a course to walk with a caddie who quickly gets your game and can guide you around the danger that is not always evident. It is a course with amazing ocean and marshland views from everywhere. And it is considered the most difficult course in the United States.

Yet, it is fair difficult. I've played it three times now and haven't broken 100, but I see that I can, if I can just put the ball on the proper side of the fairway and take smart risks appropriate for my ability. Architect Pete Dye's wife, Alice, made sure all of the tees were elevated to open up the views, and she positioned the forward tees well for the average woman player. One of the regular women visitors told me it took her a long time to break 100 there and she hasn't repeated that often yet still loves playing the Ocean Course.

As for my caddie, I believe I gained his respect when I told him where I had eaten in Charleston. "Best crabcake ever," I said, and he knew exactly where I had been — "82 Queen," he nodded. "My friend is the chef there." The heck with club selection, I just wanted that crabcake recipe. David told me he was pretty sure I could find it online, and I did.

"I'd like to have my next honeymoon here," I told him. And for once the thought did not hurt my heart. David quickly piped up, "Me too."

The night before I left Kiawah Island, I sampled both the spa and the Ocean Room in the opulent Sanctuary. Carefully I made my way down the grand staircase into the lobby, and then started a slow (dare I say, turtle-like?) stroll back to my villa. It was awfully dark and I am a bit of a klutz, but I was wearing sensible sandals and thought I could find my way along the concrete path. I walked past banquet rooms where

Casino Night was brightly lit, which perhaps made the outside walkway seem even darker and explains why I never saw the steps coming. Down I went, and stayed, awaiting rescue for what I was pretty sure, having had such klutz experiences previously, was a severely sprained ankle that quickly swelled to golf ball size. Someone brought me a cocktail as I inspected my once-pristine white slacks and saw that I would not be wearing them again.

When the resort security folks arrived, one of them asked how I fell.

"I didn't see the steps," I explained.

"What steps?" he asked.

Then, peering harder into the darkness, he finally saw what I had missed. In disgust, he smacked the tiny spotlight, about the size of a clip-on book light, that stood guard in the bushes next to the railing.

Later I learned that the resort on Kiawah has to carefully balance the needs of its guests against those of its year-round residents, the sea turtles, which mate by the light of the moon and can get confused by artificially bright light at night. Alice Dye told me that when she and Pete added the pond at 17 on the Ocean Course, one huge sea turtle grew so confused that she tried to make it her home, until rescuers steered her on a safer path.

The staff called for the next few days to check on me.

"I'm not suing anyone," I finally assured them. "Not my

style. But promise me you'll light those stairs a little better so it doesn't happen to someone else."

The pain was so severe, I wished I had crutches. Somehow the next morning I got my things down the stairs and into my little Ford Focus and drove for hours up to Charlottesville, Virginia, for my first visit to Thomas Jefferson's Monticello. I could not get around the property all that well, but seeing how this great thinker had lived lifted my spirits and ushered me outside the inner box where I had been living for the past year. When I finally tired and left there, I got lost and ended up at a nearby winery in the woods as rain began falling. A winery in the woods of Virginia, what a thing for a California wine snob to find!

My next stop would be Alexandria, Virginia, where I had lived years ago while working on the launch of *USA Today*. My first night there, I had drinks and dinner at the hotel restaurant bar and gave the bartender the wrong room number to charge. I could not remember mine — not because I had had too many drinks, but having already had three other room numbers to remember earlier on the trip.

I visited with dear old college friends and did some sightseeing in Washington, but the real reason for this particular stop was a famous painting at the Phillips Collection just outside of Georgetown. I had been reading *Luncheon of the Boating Party*, a fictionalized account of how my favorite painter, Renoir, had called on all of his friends to gather together and pose for him in a true social setting for this great work. The author did a great job of capturing the awe of the subjects in the end, when they finally saw what they had helped their friend achieve.

As I made my way through the Phillips Collection and first glimpsed *The Luncheon of the Boating Party* glowing in the distance beyond some arches, I gasped. As I neared the painting and saw the scope of its beauty, I felt a hint of the awe that must have overwhelmed his pals when they first saw it. It could have been more perfect, I thought, only if it had been *The Luncheon of the Golfing Party.*

What I have always loved about Renoir, I realized, was the way he flattered everyone and everything. I am sure his friends were not all so lustrous as *The Luncheon of the Boating Party* made them appear, but that is how his mind's eye saw them and wanted them portrayed. Every petal on a flower, every bit of skin on a fruit sparkled and gleamed under his brushes. Women, especially, glowed: you could tell he loved them.

After a year of working on the ugly, I was soothed by Renoir's rose-colored glasses and soft lens. Life had suddenly started looking kind of good, and I went across the street to a cafe where I could have a late lunch and a glass of champagne.

The table next to me was buzzing about the economic crisis. Yes, by now it was October 2008, and I was amid an uproar in the nation's capital. I looked at my Blackberry and saw that the bank where Marc and I kept our joint checking account had gone under that day.

We were insured. I just smiled and sipped my bubbly.

***

My next stop: Baltimore, where I got lots of nurturing and no blame. My parents took a ride with me one morning to Gettysburg, where an old friend from *USA Today* was general manager at a golf course. I was still limping, and a fierce wind came up, but we made our way around the 18 holes laughing at the conditions and my severe case of golf slutness. Then it was on to New York and a visit with Kristin, whom I treated to tickets to *Wicked* that I lucked into at the box office the night before the show. I had no idea that the complicated saga I had read years earlier had evolved into a story about friendship — what a treat to see it with such an old and treasured girlfriend.

I felt so transformed on the flight home, I did not do any acting out when an obese woman took over the middle seat next to me and overflowed the arm rest. Instead I cursed the airlines for not finding a way to make heavy people more comfortable.

It did occur to me, though, that I wasn't looking forward to my homecoming the way I usually did. When, back in the *Home&Garden* department, I told my editor, she said matter-of-factly, "Well, no wonder — no husband, no kids, not even a dog." She always knew how to make me laugh. I still had a job but even threw my name in for the latest round of buyouts. I'd applied once before and been turned down, and this time I withdrew my application only because it became clear I would become the paper's next Travel editor by the end of the year. I had wanted for some time to manage a features section. Friends were noticing that I seemed suddenly re-laxed.

So maybe Angela was right, and I could have put myself back on the dating market sooner instead of waiting until Jan. 4, 2009, when one separated, 5-8, curvy, 50-year-old blonde in Alameda, California, introduced herself as GottaGoGolf.

(This was before my profile-writing research revealed that "curvy," which to me sounded exotic and substantial, is a polite euphemism for "fat." I quickly downgraded myself to merely "average.")

I'm an honest, hard-working and fun-loving woman surprised to find myself single again, yet optimistic about finding a like-minded partner who's not afraid to look at himself in the mirror and look me in the eye. Friends and family say I am really really strong and also really really sweet, and so I hope to connect with some-one who will understand and appreciate both of those sides of me, and maybe have those qualities himself.

I try to take care of my health, physical and emotional, and would hope that you do the same for yourself. Bo-nus points for being literate enough to beat me at Scrab-ble and patient enough to teach me chess.

I also, you might have noticed from the headline, am a big golf nut -- a bogey golfer who wears a smile from the first tee shot to the 19th hole cocktail -- and my ideal weekend would consist of a little getaway with my guy to a pretty golf destination. Am happy on the couch too

-- an enthusiastic spectator for pro football and any kind of baseball, very adept with DVR controls so as not to miss a play or a pitch! (Betcha haven't seen too many women bragging about that sort of thing in their ads.)

I write for a living and so am not looking for long-term penpals -- would love to meet for coffee or a glass of wine and test the chemistry.

Friends I consulted — my "dating advisory board," I would come to call them — said that sounded like the best me, and a colleague at the newspaper took my camera in her hands and quickly snapped some photos that looked like the best me.

So I posted my profile and then searched for men in my age group who mentioned golf and were at least 5-foot-10. I "winked" at about 10 of them before thinking, "Enough already."

And that's how I quickly met PracticeMan and Foodie-Man, and began a journey not quite Odyssey and not quite Titanic through the contemporary world of online dating. My quest: to quickly turn a virtual meeting into a golf date.

CHAPTER FOURTEEN

Let The Games Begin

Looking for a fun and energetic person who likes adventure, but can also spend time at home enjoying quality time together. I realized recently that I have forgotten how to live life and am looking for someone to share life's experiences. I am a tad bit on the shy side, but my friends consider me humorous and fun to be around... I absolutely love golf and spending time at the range or playing around.

That was PracticeMan — note that he did not mention time actually ON the golf course, just at the range or playing "around" not playing "a round."

He swooped right in, attracted by my golf sluttism, and sent long messages about his passion for the game, his unusual heritage and family (divorced long ago and with three kids living on the East Coast) and his penchant not for playing golf but for practicing. We were having electronic conversations as we sat on our couches after work. I deemed him engineer-smart, sly-funny, and, judging from his photo, maybe a little bit too good-looking for me.

Then there was FoodieMan.

I love sunny Saturday and Sunday afternoons in the Bay Area doing something outdoors, such as wine tasting, a street festival, a jazz concert, hiking, a round of golf, exploring, or just relaxing somewhere with a view - be it people watching, great scenery, or great ambiance. I also enjoy wine country, which is pretty much the entire Bay Area and beyond these days.

Some of my greatest passions have been discovered through others' interests. So, if my partner has a passion for it, I can support and appreciate that passion, as well.

More measured in his email-and-reply routine than PracticeMan, FoodieMan would actually wait a couple of days to respond. His look and tone seemed to have an appealing warmth. He described his typical round of golf as nine holes, the perfect warmup for a fine dinner and bottle of wine.

But, when? As messages from PracticeMan and FoodieMan filled my inbox, I began to wonder, "How long does this go on?" And so when mid-January yielded a stunning weather forecast for a weekend, I emailed PracticeMan on Friday with my phone number and said, "Let's play golf on Sunday."

Just before my Saturday morning tee time with the girls, I saw a text on my Blackberry. "This is PracticeMan. Where do you want to play?"

Oh God, I thought, a text. When Marc and I were together, I expressed gratitude that I had not been single in a day and age when instant responses were possible, and even expected. We never thought of each other as instantly accessible. We knew the other would get back to us when convenient or essential.

I didn't even know how to text.

So I dialed the number.

He picked up the phone and said, "So, you want to play golf with me tomorrow, eh?"

I laughed. He said he would make us a tee time, and I got a later text with the details.

It was a cold morning, and his hug at the driving range was warm. Here I learned one of those important online dating lessons: he had used a 15-year-old picture. Maybe he thought he still looked like that. I thought he looked great at 48, chunkier and with a little less hair than that 30-something but still with the beautiful brown eyes, dark wavy hair, and shy smile. Heck, he might have been younger than 30 in the picture — I just know that when I asked him during the round about the significance of that earring he was wearing in the profile photo, he said, "Oh, I haven't worn an earring in 15 years." It was such a hunky photo that a friend who had been dating online for years looked at it and gasped. "You just went online for the first time and you met this?" she said. I had to tell her, yes, but he doesn't look like that anymore, he looks good, just not like that.

It was my first date in, oh, 12 years. Yet I felt safe, and

calm, and very unselfconscious — and I know that's because we were on a golf course, where there were plenty of people around, yet I did not have to compete with perfectly assembled women and worry about my hat hair. I was on my home turf, literally.

There was a moment of awkwardness in the pro shop, where I intended to pay my green fee yet PracticeMan firmly held out his credit card to the starter and gave a glare that said, "On me." I knew he made big bucks and had a great living arrangement (with Mom), but I still appreciated this chivalrous gesture — one I would remember on later dates as others did all they could to avoid being the first to check in at the cash register.

PracticeMan seemed a little bit shy, just as advertised, and I had a little trouble reading his attraction and interest because he seemed to go out of his way not to touch me. But as the day went on, he seemed so comfortable that after a few holes we even told the two friendly fellows with whom we'd been paired that it was our first meeting.

He had a beautiful, well-practiced golf swing, and no temper at all. When we arrived at a drivable par-4 and he started to reach for an iron to make a safe play in the middle of the fairway, I suggested he take a shot with his driver.

"It's just a recreational round," I told him. "You've been hitting the ball great. I think you could get there."

He did! His tee shot rolled to the back of the green and he three-putted for par. I'm guessing he told his buddies about that.

The date ended with a hug, and with some messaging later on. He admired my golf shoes but wondered how I'd manage in stilettos. I said, "I am a klutz and wouldn't want to walk in them, however, they might be appropriate in some places." He messaged back, "Barefoot is fine."

Meanwhile, I went to meet FoodieMan for happy hour in San Francisco. We carefully chose a hotel lounge that appeared to offer a great deal on food and drink, yet would allow for easy conversation rather than requiring elbowing up to the bar. His face was the smiling version of his serious photo, with a fast-receding hairline, precisely groomed beard, curious eyes, and the kind of facial lines that have been etched in smiles and laughter. FoodieMan became a prototype for the typical online encounter: I liked him, I had a great, fun time with him, and then I went home thinking about PracticeMan and wondering if he was still awake and online for some messaging.

In FoodieMan's case, I actually hoped to have a second meeting, but our schedules were not aligned and we faded away. This, too, was prototypical of the pretty good first meeting. A second meeting is discussed but never comes to fruition.

PracticeMan and I had a fun evening outing at the driving range later in the week, and I started wondering when first kiss comes into play in the online dating world. PracticeMan seemed big on analysis, not so big on taking a leap. He told me about a setup his sister had attempted that he had decided not to pursue because the woman seemed too flaky. It was a Seinfeld show, with nothing happening after a whole lot of discussion about something happening. It was a lot of reading of the green without resulting in the act of putting.

I suppose he would have spent more time considering me and less time meeting me, except that I impatiently invited him out for another round of golf the next weekend. Afterward, over alfresco lunch on a patio overlooking vineyards, something seemed off, until I told him about my outing with FoodieMan, and he said, "You met someone else? After we started emailing?" I nodded uncertainly, thinking, isn't that what people do on Match? Don't they meet possible matches in search of an actual match? Don't they do some dating, then begin to focus on one in particular, maybe fall in love, go exclusive, then plan a future together?

I quickly told him that when the date ended I was looking forward to coming home and emailing him, but in retrospect I realized he never really looked me in the eye again. He was "too tired" to meet on my couch that evening to share a bottle of wine we had picked out. I thought, uh oh, maybe that's that.

He was texting me again the next day while I hosted friends to watch pro football, so I told myself not to overreact. "You're just out of practice," the whole-hearted Susan said to the broken-hearted one whose hand she held. "Be positive, don't overanalyze."

The next day, he stunned me with a break-up email that said he did not feel a romantic connection with me although he liked me and hoped we could be friends and play golf together.

I did not react well to this. It seemed so unnecessary and cruel — all he had to do was stop texting and messaging me every day and I would understand. He had been the one in daily pursuit for two and a half weeks, yet now felt he had to rebuff me? I was insulted and hurt.

I told him I had plenty of friends and thank you. When I saw him one day weeks later on the putting green (just practicing, of course), I gave him a big smile and wave. And as he took a step in my direction, I kept walking.

As ambivalent as I felt about *The Rules of Golf*, I started wishing for a similarly complicated yet universal *Rules of Dating* that would apply to all. Without it, we were left to ourselves to first discern and then observe the etiquette — and etiquette, new women golfers well know, has a steep learning curve and lines that blur according to the company.

There's the mulligan, and the question of when to offer one to a man without seeming to insult his virility. Then there are the long minutes waiting in the fairway from 250 yards out because if he connects with his three-wood the way he did that one day at the driving range when he was 14, he will cold-cock someone in the foursome now on the green. (A golfing woman friend calls this common, curiously male phenomenon "delusions of grandeur.")

There is also the question of when to offer and accept a "gimme," a golf term not in *The Rules of Golf* but now as commonly used as "slam dunk" in everyday conversation. The rules require each player to putt out until the ball hits the bottom of the cup, except in match play, where the scoring is based not on final stroke totals but on the result at each hole. In match play, one may concede a putt that hardly matters by saying, "That's good." Some players concede every putt inside three or four feet until there are only a few holes left in the match; then they become mute. That's a strategy based on the theory that someone who has not had to make a short putt for 15 holes might tense up over a two-footer on the 16th and miss.

In your everyday recreational round, though, etiquette justifies picking up a putt so close to the hole that it is considered unmissable. The "delusions of grandeur" phenomenon tends to come into play with men, whose gimme range may be as long as five or six feet. Play with a group of women, and it is five or six inches. Put the genders together, and now we have grounds for confusion and even some hard feelings. The women will say, "The nerve of that guy, picking up all his six-footers and then saying he shot 79." And the men will say, "We'd have finished an hour earlier if only she hadn't agonized over all those two-foot putts. After all, I told her they were good!"

Ultimately it is the player who has to decide what is good. How much generosity is to be accepted before it is deemed condescension? The answer can vary with every round, depending on the company and the stakes. Even the etiquette of where to stand and when to talk transcends the rulebook. Fill in for a friend in her regular weekday foursome and you may find conversation that flows from address to backswing to follow-through. Are you really going to try to shush them? In my bright orange pants once in a tournament, an overstimulated fellow competitor continually asked me to move so that I was nowhere in her sight when she played a shot. I would not have broken any rules or violated any manners had I stayed put, but on that day I obliged whenever I could.

I had to Google to learn contemporary dating etiquette. Weekend dates should be made by Wednesday, or singles ought to make other plans (or at least say they did). Men who would like a second date with a woman should call or otherwise touch base the day after the first; women who would like a second date with a man should do nothing. It seemed to me that men had it so easy if they did not want a second date. They could say and do nothing. Women who did not want a second date with a man who did were going to have to say or do something.

Away from the course, PracticeMan had given me my first lesson in rejection etiquette: everyone has a method or style, and some are kinder than others. I was going to have to find my own way, too, I would learn. Because sometimes the mismatch would be clearly mutual and we would just not reconnect. Sometimes we would concur in a friendly manner that, hey, this is not a match but it has been fun; I actually have made friends that way.

But other times, either I or my match had more enthusiasm than the other. A disinterested man had only to not follow up — a woman savvy about etiquette would get that. Suppose I was the disinterested one? An enthusiastic man rarely waits for a woman to follow up; he's been trained to pursue. So I learned to email first thing the next morning (not that evening, that would be just too rude) to say, "I had a great time last night and thought you were a great shuffleboard companion. Something tells me that we are not a match, for whatever reason, and I have learned not to ignore it when I get that 'something tells me' impulse. I know you are going to find a fantastic match and wish you the best."

One nonprospect, admittedly a little bit overweight, never took off his yellow slicker during a mellow wine tasting on a rainy Sunday evening. Now, I am not that picky about a man's looks, but he's got to feel good about himself and his body. He also claimed complete ignorance about why his wife of 25 years suddenly, abruptly, shockingly decided she no longer wanted to be married to him. It was a mystery! (Men, don't be clueless.)

Another engaged me in a long, introspective exchange of over-worded emails before he finally admitted, "Oh, by the way, I am married but am exploring the alternatives. Just thought you should know." (Guys, there's a thing called "separation" that is ideal for the low-risk adventure cruise.) I played golf with him anyway but even this golf slut couldn't really get past his dating etiquette violation.

Yet another complimented me on what a kind and positive rejection I had learned to give. He apparently liked them so much, he'd come back every few weeks for a time to receive another.

After a few pleasant dates that went nowhere, I connected with a man who claimed to love wine and golf. We talked on the phone, and I was impressed — an engineer, close to his former stepdaughters, a member of the Olympic Club in San Francisco, works out there every day. He sounded so smart, so normal, so pleasant. Two conversations later we were making a golf date.

"I made a tee-time for Saturday at nine," I told OlympicMan. "I'll meet you at the course."

"I'd rather meet on the way to the course so we can go together," he said. "I've never been there before. You can show me the way, and we can have some time to talk."

OlympicMan did live in another city, but this struck me as odd in the age of Mapquest and GPS. Inviting him to pick me up at my home would have been an etiquette violation warranting a two-stroke penalty in online-dating first meetings, so I chose a neutral spot, as my advisory board suggested, a coffee house en route to the same course where I had played with PracticeMan.

I was there having coffee and a muffin, waiting. Finally, in walked a very wide man, wearing glasses and a crooked toupe. He smiled at me.

Aha.

I almost asked, "Have you seen OlympicMan, the togeth-er-looking businessman in the photo?" But my wheels were spinning. I realized quickly why he had wanted to pick me up; he no doubt had had the experience of being spotted in a busy place by a date who had left without ever acknowledg-ing him.

I loaded my clubs into his SUV and we motored to the course.

"Together or separate?" asked the starter in the pro shop.

"Separate," said OlympicMan, handing over his credit card.

During the round, I learned that he was a member not of the U.S Open host Olympic Club golf club but of its down-town athletic club. He had used a photo of perhaps 20 years earlier, when the hair might have been real and the body 50 pounds lighter. He was an engineer, but did not have a job. He played golf, but oh-so-badly.

OlympicMan had created a work of fiction in order to get a real date with me. Either that or this was the dating equivalent of the golf course phenomenon "delusions of grandeur." But even if he believed the things he had told me were true, or had been at one time, or would be someday, I wondered how quickly he realized the jig was up? I suspect it was at that point near the ninth green, when I looked around wondering where he had gone off to in the golf cart. Suddenly I felt a sharp pain in my right breast. I looked down, where a golf ball had struck me and fallen to the ground. I looked around, and there was OlympicMan, far away on an adjacent fairway, watching in dismay as his shot into the green found a target that he never would.

By now, his manmade hair had blown sideways under his hat, and we both took a breather at the turn to hit the restroom. As I waited in the cart for him to reassemble, I took a few deep breaths (and rubbed my boob). Then I did my part to be pleasant company and (figuratively) lie in the bed that I had made. After all, I was playing golf.

In the end, I played his game. "Let's do this again sometime!" I said, warmly I thought. He looked surprised. I think he even said, "Really?" and I replied, again feigning sincerity, "Oh, yes!" Once I had been returned to my car in front of the coffee shop, I gave him a big hug before jumping in and locking the door.

I figured I was just reciprocating what he had offered me.

Of course, the more I thought about it later, the angrier I felt. What was the point of such misrepresentation? To get a date, okay, I get that. But any potential for an honest relationship already has been undermined. How does one expect to go from, "I lied about my golf game, what I look like, how old I am, what I do, and what I like to do," to, "I, OlympicMan, promise to love you forever," or even the possibility of an exclusive committed relationship? Or even sex? Now I understood why some matches put in their profiles in capital letters "EVERYTHING IN MY PROFILE IS TRUE AND MY PHOTOS ARE RECENT, PLEASE DO THE

SAME." Apparently fiction had become such a bestseller on Match.com that truth-tellers felt the need to make their profiles stand out.

My day with OlympicMan had seemed so long and unnecessary, I stopped to rethink the whole concept of golf-as-18-holes. After all, in the game's early days, a golf course had as few as six holes and more typically 12 holes. Then the church of golf, Scotland's St. Andrews, started messing around with its layout, and by the late 1800s, 18 became standard pretty much by accident. The widely held theory that golf is a game of 18 holes because a bottle of scotch holds 18 shots obviously holds no water — because then water is all we would have left for the important 19th hole.

I hear the Scots play the game more briskly than we do in the States — maybe because the weather is often not the kind in which a golfer wants to linger, it's the kind that propels their arses quickly around the links and into the warm, waiting bar. If they had known, back in the 1800s, that Americans would take five or six hours to play 18, perhaps the famous St. Andrews clock atop the clubhouse might have been converted into a timer that stopped each round at precisely four hours, no matter the hole. Three hours, even — that, I think, would be the ticket for converting the occasional recreational golfer into the unabashed golf slut.

That a marathon — at 26 miles, 385 yards, an odd distance attributable, like our 18, to a bit of random quirkiness

in the United Kingdom — can be run by the average contest-
ant in less time than it takes the best player to play 18 holes
of golf does not serve The Game well.

This is all the more torturous with the wrong companions. Most of the women I know who play golf have a tale or
two to tell about wrong companions, and they are usually
men. Often torture starts with the preconceptions brought
to the first tee. A woman golf professional I know tells of the
morning she and a friend — both of them hung over from a
bachelorette party the night before — headed for the first tee.
It was supposed to be a fun round, so one said to the other,
"Let's just play from the red tees today." The other agreed.
"That's probably as much as I can handle this morning," she
said.

Along came their companions, two men they had not
met. And one of them said, "Girls, let's just try to keep up."
The "girls" eyeballed each other, stepped back to their regular
white tees to tee off, and put the men to shame with their
long drives and par-neighborhood scoring.

Both twosomes might have had fun, but I suspect they
did not have fun with each other. Having played often with
guys and with girls, I took a poll once of my men friends to
find out, "What are the assumptions you make when you are
paired to play with women?" One or two of them quickly
fired back emails to say, "I'm sure not going to tell you, of all
people." Others delivered me quite the varied list of myths,
truths, and myths I wished were true.

They said they had to watch their language. That doesn't

seem like such a bad thing. But don't they feel ludicrous doing that when we women are uttering, "Shit, I suck," before we've gotten off the first tee?

They said the wife doesn't like cigar smoking, and now here they are playing with women who don't like it either. Why is cigar smoking socially acceptable and even encouraged in golf when we have successfully spun cigarettes into nasty, shameful habits? I think cigar smoke is gross and inescapable. Once, though, I politely asked if a cigar smoker would mind please not smoking his stogie at the putting green, and he answered, "But that's when I need it most."

They said their wives might be jealous. So, encourage the wife to play too.

They said they would be distracted by legs, breasts, eyes, etc. Well...

They said women talk too much. I think probably that's a fair generalization, and when I play with someone who talks a four-round into a four-and-a-half-hour round, she's not going to be at the top of my call list for a free round at Pebble Beach.

They also said we worry about "stuff that doesn't matter," which I think is generally true when we play with men, because we're worried about what they think of us, whether we're observing proper etiquette, and whether our game is embarrassing us.

They said they like to compete and women don't, which I think is generally true because when I play with men there is almost always a wager of some kind and with women there almost never is.

One said it bothered him that women get to play "the ladies' tee" even though they are better than him. Here's where
ego comes into play in a round of golf with men. Tee boxes
do not have genitals. When you think about it, all of the tees
are ladies' tees. And all of the tees are men's tees. My golf pro
bachelorette party friend should never play from the most
forward (usually red) tees, because her game is too long for
them. My man friend who has a spinal cord injury should
always play the most forward tees because his distance is
about the same as mine, a little better than average for a typical woman. Yet, when we play a match from the forward
tees, where we are quite equally matched by our handicaps,
the USGA handicap system requires that Phil give me a
stroke or two because he is a man and those tees are rated
easier for men than for women. Phil and I know that's not
right, but we haven't figured out a fix to offer the USGA. Or,
we'd call, before our next match.

When I gave a talk to a women's golf group and shared
with them what men had told me about playing with wom-
en, I asked them about their assumptions when they are
paired with men.

Men, the golf gals observed in disgust, will urinate anywhere on the golf course, even when there is a rest room a
pitching wedge away. Sometimes, if it's occupied, they will
even urinate ON the rest room. When I have asked men
(not in mid-stream, of course) why they do this, they answer, "Because I can." Unfortunately many golf courses are

laid out in such a way that one may be required to urinate anywhere, despite having paid $100 for a four-to-five-hour pursuit for which we have probably all dressed up in pricey clothes and shoes. We've got easier access to defibrillators these days than toilets. Women can't help but have penis envy at about the 16th hole.

The golf gals also complained that men play from the wrong tees. "Why is that horrible hacker playing back there from the Tiger tees?" That is so true that on a typical day many golf courses do not place tees on the boxes they've designed for superior players because they don't want Harry Hacker to go back there and, as he will say, "experience the whole golf course." It would be so much better (for all of us) for Harry Hacker to experience fairways and greens rather than ponds and forests.

Finally, and perhaps accordingly, the women said, men play too slow. Well, really, how fast can a guy move when he's hitting from the wrong tees, fishing balls out of hazards, and urinating all over the place? C'mon gals, let's give him a break. I think women say men are slow because they think the men are saying women are slow. In fact, I believe women are more conscious about their pace of play and men are more conscious about their egos. Men also seem to think that if they spend more time tossing grass into the air, pacing off yardages and remembering swing tips, they will have a better result. I would like to see some statistics on the likelihood of success with a practice swing versus without. Only then will I start to take one routinely.

However long it takes, the golf slut of course should be grateful for the minutes spent on a golf course and not working, parenting, or, ugh!, dating.

It's the combining of golf and dating that can encroach on one's sense of gratitude. Six holes, 12 holes, 18 holes — whatever the final verdict of the Royal and Ancient of St. Andrews — one can argue that any number was more than I needed to see through OlympicMan.

So the next seemingly good-looking and successful man who connected with me, who described himself as a single-digit handicapper, I met on one chilly March afternoon just to hit some balls and do a bit of putting. Tall, blond, and fit, he was justifiably proud of the business he had grown and the daughter he had raised. We had a little bit of competitive fun, with a hit-the-can contest that he won going away and a putt-off in which I narrowly prevailed, and when at the end he said, "Let's play golf sometime," I felt I had passed a test. He was someone I would like to get to know better.

Then I received his next email — "I booked a tee time tomorrow with a buddy, why don't you just show up and play with us?" I couldn't make it, or the next unromantic quasi-invitation, or the next, and LukeWarmMan disappeared down the drain. I wondered if, judging by LukewarmMan's unromantic follow-through, I had compromised my femininity by winning the putting contest? Not wise, maybe, but at least it was honest. There's no fakery in golf, which has been described as a game of honor because we're supposed to keep our own scores, call our own penalties, and report our own rules violations. I felt pretty certain that my own profile and photos represented me accurately, I just wasn't quite connecting with anyone in the way I had hoped and expected.

Monday morning, March 23, I flew east to collect several travel stories and attend a conference, first with a visit to my family in Baltimore. At work, another fierce round of buyouts was under way with the kind of compensation many thought would never be offered again. I printed out my paperwork in case I decided while I was on my trip that I should once again apply to leave the newspaper.

CHAPTER FIFTEEN

Interpreter Please

The trip home had taken a dark turn. My vigorous, golf-loving cousin Tom had died of a fast cancer, only in his mid 60s. We had always talked about playing golf together and never did. My itinerary would put me there for the funeral.

While I packed, an email arrived via the free dating site I had just joined, Plenty of Fish. And soon I was laughing.

Well, here is me in a nut house... I mean, in a nutshell.

I was born in a Latin country and am of Asian descent. I speak several languages, look younger than my age, and am a true gentleman. I am open-minded, intelligent, honest, reliable, trustworthy, caring, a communicator. Also have a wonderful sense of humor and am fun to be with. If you are my complete opposite, do hit the back button. I will be open to anything you want to throw at me; lamentably, I take exception to cutlery, pots, microwaves, laptops, etc.

I participate in all sports and have just taken up golf. I

lift weights six days a week and I only run when I am being chased or if I have to chase after you. I snow ski badly, dance like it is nobody's business, and sing like a dying cat.

I enjoy wine tasting up in Napa Valley and would someday love to drive up to the wine country with my partner and have a picnic on the grounds of those beautiful vineyards. I own a Lamborghini and love to drive it fast. I don't drive crazy, just fast. I must share that it does not have an "Oh Jesus" bar and the hand brake doesn't qualify as one. If you do not like occasional speed, I am sorry, but you are not the one for me. Since I do enjoy driving fast and I am directionally challenged, if I happen to miss our turn, please refrain from saying "Didn't you see the arrow?" Sorry, no; I didn't even see the bloody Indians.

I have two lovely daughters who live nearby with their mother. If you do not have any kids, you are certainly welcome to mine. I work in San Francisco for a tech startup.

Thank you for reading, I trust that I at least put a smile on your face. May I ask of you, respectfully, not to stereotype, label, or categorize me, just get to know me?

My loquacious new pen pal had an exotic look — shaved head and face, almond eyes, seemingly slight of build. Though a year or two older than me, he looked much younger, in fact, and so I probably would not have initiated a dialog. When he did and I reciprocated, whew, there seemed to be a lot to say — and, while I was in Washington D.C. for that travel writers conference, we gave our fingers a rest and went to the phones, until those started to die off too.

He knew very little about golf, I quickly learned, because he had taken my 19th hole reference in my own profile to mean sex. I wrote back:

I think you have been miseducated. The 19th hole is drinks. Then if that goes well one might have dinner, the 20th hole. If all of that went really well, perhaps there would be a 21st hole.

His embarrassed apology gave us a running joke we could take to the driving range — because, it turned out, Bond-Man's game wasn't quite ready for even 18 holes.

We had a half-century of catching-up to do before we met, on everything from treasured values to family backgrounds to favorite movies. BondMan idolized 007, the womanizing fictional character with great survival instincts, and the powerful sports car in his garage might have hinted at a penchant for risk, except that he had a fairly normal job, lived in a nondescript neighborhood of modest homes, and commuted in a Ford Taurus. He had not had a ticket since he was 19. So I comfortably confided in him as it became more and more clear that I should seek a buyout in my job of 15 years. Back in the office, I learned, most of my colleagues were leaving. At the end of every day came an email praising so-and-so's illustrious career of oh-so-many years, then, there would be two and three of those emails from different managers. I received calls from panicked editors asking if I'd agree to take over the *Home&Garden* section, then when I seemed uninterested in that, more calls assuring me that I could continue on as *Travel* Editor, even though my budget would be cut and I'd lose my staff of one.

If I passed up the buyout, I realized, I would have to do whatever they wanted me to do. I liked my editors and felt I belonged among them, or could at least keep up with them on the golf course. But I finally had the job I wanted, and who knows for how long if I stayed. This was my chance to leave on my own terms, taking along a comfortable cushion. I could even take a few months completely off, work on my golf game, go to Hawaii, and figure out what to do with my skills.

Or I could stay until I really just had to get out, and leave with nothing.

My college friends thought it was a no-brainer and time for me to go. Older friends and family members thought it was no time to give up a job.

The eight-hour drive from Washington down to Kiawah Island gave me plenty of time to think and an excuse not the answer phone calls. Soon after I arrived, I went over to the resort's executive offices and sent a fax to the newspaper's human resources department requesting an extension on the deadline to finalize my decision until I was able to return and speak to my supervisors.

BondMan didn't question my judgment during the long phone call one rainy night just before I would play the Ocean Course a second time. It was raining so hard, though, I might not have heard him clearly. It rained so much that week, the Banyons, visiting from Copperopolis, opted out of the discounted round I had arranged and decided to leave the island. So I headed over the course by myself, feeling a bit forlorn and sure it would be slow-rolling and sloppy.

But the Ocean Course sits on a sand base, and at the end of the glorious day of escape from the stress of a life decision, I noticed that my pants legs were clean and my chest was sunburned. It didn't rain that day and the course did not show signs of any soaking. I left there no longer undecided about leaving the paper, instead thinking, "What kind of business can I start that will bring me back here?"

Back at the office, my editor seemed not just amenable but appreciative when I asked if I could stay around until August and then leave with the buyout. "Stay as long as you want," he said. "We don't want you to leave."

More to my surprise, BondMan seemed to be in no hurry to meet before then! He called to make sure I had gotten home safely, and then told me all about his weekend plans with his daughters. He lived a good 45 minutes away from me and headed for work so early in the morning that he got up at 3:45 every day to work out.

Maybe I had finally met one of those men who only date virtually and not really, I thought. I had heard of this.

So I met another suitor for a quick after-work drink near the paper. I was dressed for a charity function at a show house; he was wearing a T-shirt and jeans, and though he knew my full name did not appear to have Googled my background. It was the longest hour in my dating portfolio, though he seemed like a perfectly nice guy and subsequently emailed for a mulligan more quickly than I could deliver my "you seem like a great guy but something tells me we are not a match" message.

I just did not see the point to a mulligan here. Instead, I manufactured a travel story outing to the wine country for two and sent BondMan the itinerary at the beginning of the week. He okayed it.

It started at his house. After all, we already knew each other, right? I knew his first and last names, his address, his phone number, where he worked, his daughters' names and schools. I felt safe enough to rendezvous there for our day.

And so I was. But, as all of the do's and don'ts of online dating will tell you, you do not know someone with whom you have only emailed and telephoned. If you forget this, you will be reminded by your friends who have dated virtually. Until you meet, there is no actual relationship. I prepared myself for him not to be attracted to me, or vice versa.

I thought he was adorable — taller than I expected, and broader, quite firm from those wee-hours workouts. I thought he at first seemed nervous and pleased with me. "Okay, this is going to be fun," he said with some relief. But, as the day went on, I noticed the way his arm came up between us when he was sitting next to me, the way he'd look down in his lap instead of over at me.

It was okay, I thought, as we drove home in his fast car from a wonderful day that had started with a wine and cheese tasting at a winery high on a hilltop and ended with a flight of reds on a picnic bench under an oak tree in the back yard of an antique shop. He had driven a nice car and been fine company, and I hadn't jumped to premature conclusions that rendered the day a disappointment. I didn't need to analyze his apparent lack of attraction to me.

But then as we made our way out of the wine country, it seemed he didn't want the day to end. He invited me to his favorite neighborhood pizza place, and so it was dark when we got back to my car. Before I could give him a friendly goodbye hug, he leaned in for a kiss.

Though this pleasantly surprised me, it also confused me. I thought he had been delivering another message.

BondMan and I would have more time together, during which I would notice that the less available I was, the more interested he was. We went to the driving range, but one trip to the golf course for nine holes proved premature — he was not a golfer, as athletic as he seemed to think of himself, and had no understanding of rules and etiquette. I encouraged him as best I could — setting him up with a golf bag, and a club I did not use that he hit straight and true. At one tournament where I was a guest that summer, Nike gave all of the participants money to spend in its pro shop, and I ordered BondMan a pair of shoes in the latest swoosh style.

Unfortunately, he had no tolerance for being adored, and told me that his one serious relationship since his divorce had ended because she seemed to be a little too into him. His inferiority complex came to life as he spoke bitterly about the stereotypes about Asian men — stereotypes I knew nothing about. I Googled: Asian men are supposed to be sort of effeminate, and, in the extreme stereotype, have small penises. No kidding! I did not carry around a ruler, but none of this seemed to apply to BondMan, not that I cared about any stereotypes at all. My Mr. Right qualifications had never had a hair color (though I did have a preference for hair), skin tone (though I loved a tan), or language (though I hoped to understand it).

It didn't matter what I thought, though. I was not going to convince a man who thought himself unworthy of being adored that he was adorable.

Early one Saturday morning, walking the golf course with pals from the newspaper, I realized that I was not feeling the love of this romance, and that I was not disposed to handle a lot of uncertainty in life right now. I wish I did, I wish I could, but, blinking back tears, I felt I could not.

When I went home and emailed BondMan about this, I immediately wanted to unpush the SEND button. After all, I told myself, we had played a very long golf course that morning — maybe it had just exhausted me to the point of stupidity.

But then, his response:

If I may be so bold in saying that you will make someone an amazing partner. I must share that I enjoy having quite a few friends to do things with and not be tied

down to any. This way there will be no expectation of anyone but the overall goal of having a fabulous time... I am sorry that you were thinking one way and I had other ideas.

I steamed, feeling a little bit silly. The golf shoes arrived a week later, and I stowed them in the back of the coat closet.

I renewed my Match.com membership for a month and sent "MORE THAN A WINK" to a dark-eyed attorney who said he liked golf.

In return, I received a very articulately delivered lecture.

RE: MORE THAN A WINK

Thank you for your kind words and pleasant email. You sound like someone I would like to know and you appear attractive in your photos.

My concern is that your status shows "Currently Separated." I have been on and off Match for several years and dated a few people. I have not met any women who were only separated who were actually ready for a serious relationship. Many of them THOUGHT they were ready, but found out they weren't. Most people who are separated, the last thing on their mind is remarrying! I am not looking for a dating relationship, I am seeking someone for a much more serious commitment. You are still going through important steps in your divorce/breakup that minimize your ability to love, share, engage in intimacy, etc. I want to be with a woman who not only has healed, but is enthusiastic about pur-

suing a close, loving relationship, WITHOUT any needi-iness, emotional desperation, or draining insecurities. Those people do not work for me, as I have already learned. In other words, why pursue a relationship when I know from experience that the odds are stacked against its success? Recently separated people who were married for many years tend to be very poor risks for long-term love since they do not even realize they must go through a long healing process.

I think we are on different pages here. Best wishes to you.

This email, so convincingly penned by a professional arguer, stuck in my brain, and I had to ask a few friends, "Am I not ready, still?" They mostly laughed at me. We agreed I was completely, definitely, healthily separated and doing pretty well. Marc and I weren't talking unless we had business to discuss; I had no idea how he was really doing, and though I hoped that someday we would be able to talk to each other in a caring way, right now we both had to find our new way of life. I had a career change to navigate — and on top of that, the rental house was on the market and I would probably have to move, which meant I should start thinking about finding a new place to live while I still had steady income to write on the applications.

All of this seemed more opportunity than obstacle to me. I loved my job and my home but believed these changes were going to be taking me farther away from the life I had had with Marc, a life I could not have again, toward a new life with someone else. So I welcomed them.

But, especially after my dryly funny round with SarcasmMan, who had seemed to want so desperately to beat me and put me in my place, I began to think LegalEagle had a point and I hadn't yet reached a point of seriousness. Congratulations to me for having learned enough over the course of five months to recognize, pre-meeting, that SarcasmMan was no match for me. But shame on me for putting us both through 19 holes of needless misery, starting with offering a mulligan at the first tee.

By now, I had tried Match.com, Plenty of Fish, and even Craigslist, where the personals are free and the resulting scene can only be described as a free-for-all. I had even met a setup offered by friends. He was a surgeon, had his own plane, loved to fly off to this golf course or that one, and had put a healthy amount of time between himself and his last girlfriend. She, they told me, was way too young for him.

I saw no pictures and simply exchanged a few good-humored emails before SingleDoc and I made a date to meet at a wine bar. "I've heard a lot of good things about that place," he emailed. As I walked up, there he was out front — pleasant enough looking, asking if we could go somewhere else because he could not drink wine.

Martinis? Those, he could drink.

Here is what I remember about the date: He had hurt one body part in a car accident. He had hurt another body part in a skiing accident. He also had a health condition that required that he medicate.

I felt that not only his last girlfriend was way too young for him — even I was. His presentation skills definitely needed work. (Men: if you are interested in a woman, you do not want to spend your first date hinting at all of the reasons you are likely to be incapacitated for the rest of your life.)

I would have liked to have had another date. Maybe he was just nervous. He emailed to say he would be in touch when he was ready to play golf again.

I do have a goal of having my body ready for a game by the time you're off work.

That was June. I was leaving my job in August.

Last I heard from my friends, SingleDoc was still getting in shape for me. Maybe he still is!

CHAPTER SIXTEEN

Match Fatigue

The divorce was final in July, on August 24 I moved into an apartment on the Oakland waterfront, and on August 28 I hurried out of the newspaper offices for the last time after my mostly wonderful 15 years with the *Chronicle* and *Examiner*.

Golf made it especially difficult to leave. For a couple of years, a colleague had been telling me about the publisher's passion for the game and encouraged me to get out and play with him. I came from a blue-collar family and had been a longtime union member, however, and I perceived Frank as a bottom line guy who didn't care about the little people like me. Then my old friend Ward became editor of the paper, and he lured me into a Saturday outing at the Presidio, the old military post in San Francisco with its sneaky, tree-lined and usually fog-covered layout that occasionally offered a city vista. It's so reliably cold there that chili may outsell hot dogs at the turn.

When I checked in at the counter, I told the pro how nervous I was about playing with my bosses. He said, "Don't be nervous, just don't beat them."

At the first tee, the three guys I was playing with asked each other, "Should we have a match?" And their consensus was, "Nah, Frank's not here, let's just play golf."

So we just played golf and it was wonderful. Ward is a big strong guy who hits the ball far — and sometimes wide. His second in command revered golf so much that he gobbled up historic accounts and biographies, and had collected vintage clubs that he would use on occasion. The two of them had good rounds, in the mid 80s.

Our third that day was an ad executive with a drawl worthy of Augusta National and a more creative game than any of us is likely to see again. He hit driver off the tee, and then hit driver again off the fairway or from wherever he could not figure out what else to do. By now I understood that most of us make the game much more complicated than "get the ball into the hole," and I thought, how smart this man was to replace the decision between three or four clubs with his commitment to one. I actually got a big laugh once out of a friend who had lost an arm, because when we were discussing how he managed to swing a golf club, I said, "Maybe you're lucky — you've got fewer body parts to screw up in the golf swing than the rest of us do." He gave me one of those "Did you really say that?" looks and then roared. "I really hadn't thought about it that way before," he said.

At the Presidio, the one-club man shot 98, and I shot a

steady 95. When I remarked later what a nice, mellow, friendly round the four of us had had, they agreed but said somewhat dismissively, "Oh, well, but Frank's not here." So when I played with them again and Frank was there, I had visions of a frenzied exhibition of profanity and club-throwing.

Frank won me over by first picking up my green fee before I arrived. Then he bought me a margarita on the second fairway. (It was not even 9 a.m.) By the time we reached the second green, he had cajoled me into a wager — no doubt not giving me as many strokes as I deserved (but, he had paid) — and we had a very courteous and competitive round. I am sure he won — at least I hope so (because, after all, he had paid).

Frank has a killer short game and is an expert putter, which makes up for his lack of length off the tee. Indeed, only Ward had a long game — the rest of us scraped and scrambled, a condition that most of us accepted but not Frank. I've never seen anyone so regularly dissatisfied with his game — and, I've been told, he would indeed misbehave if I wasn't there — yet when he was on he was so full of glee that we all had to root for him to have a good day. He was a real guy, and over those months of golfing with him I learned a lot about the challenges he had to overcome in the publishing business — not the least of which were the seemingly endless buyouts and layoffs at the *Chronicle*. He prided himself on caring about little people like me, had friends (he made sure I knew) who were union members and did not consider him a union buster, and I would not ever have come to known him had we not shared this passion for golf. I declare Frank my fellow golf slut, and I suspect he is going to proudly show this to his friends.

Frank's wife, by the way, once complimented me for being able to hang with the guys over the course of 18 holes. She had had enough after 11 or 12. Other wives, and women in the office, seemed not at all jealous but echoed her admiration for how I had come to be welcome in the inner circle. I thought that was pretty neat, on the one hand; on the other, I could see how the inner circle's golf-based camaraderie might extend sexist hiring practices and gender-based cronyism.

Some weeks we had two foursomes, so there would be seven guys plus me. I felt privileged to be invited back week after week — especially when I got to play with a high-level company executive whose name I had seen often in corporate announcements out of New York over the years. We had a great talk along the way about him recently having remarried after his wife of many years had died.

I know that these men saw qualities in me that applied in the workplace as well as on the golf course. I didn't waste time, I followed the rules they established, I maintained an optimistic outlook, I welcomed coaching, I tried not to talk too much, but I did my best to smile a lot. We did not talk about work endlessly — in fact, one tip I would give women playing business golf is, don't bring up business. A few more: put your makeup on before the round, stay sober, and freshen up your hair before sitting down to the 19th hole. Work will come up, and you want to look professional and competent when it does. And if they do invite you in on a wager, go ahead and take their money along with every stroke and distance advantage they will allow — then be prepared to buy the drinks and gloat.

It became harder to leave the newspaper because I realized these were people I really wanted to work for. As August 28 approached, I worked at home as much as I could and avoided reminders of how much I would miss my golf guys.

I tried not to say goodbye to anyone on the last day, as I got my things together and turned over my keys and credentials. But carrying a box down the hall, I crossed paths with Leah Garchik, the classy and gracious columnist of many years for the features department. "It has been such a privilege," I began. Then, I started swallowing so hard, nothing would come out. We nodded at each other and I left the building. Later there was a call from Ward, who seemed to understand when I told him that I could not possibly go and say goodbye to him in his fishbowl of an office, where I'd be blubbering away for anyone to see.

Anyway, I had a tee time with BareChestMan. We'd been emailing and talking on the phone at length for a couple of weeks, after I'd "favorited" him (a Plenty of Fish thing) and sent him a greeting.

I usually flip right past the guys who have their shirts off, but in your case I realized you were doing something you loved (swimming in the ocean) and so I got over myself. Plus you look pretty good!

BareChestMan was not at all the typical poser; he put a lot of thought into everything he did and how it would affect the people around him. We talked quite a bit about his work issues managing construction projects, and I liked the way he got over himself and dealt directly with his colleagues. I found it endearing rather than imposing when he had started texting me every morning on his way to work sites and calling or emailing most evenings.

BareChestMan practiced yoga and mindfulness. Googling him got me nowhere, but Googling the tenets of his philosophy took me somewhere I needed to be during that time of so much change. He got me reading all about "The Laws of Attraction," and thinking about what I really wanted and whether I believed it was possible.

"Somewhere in your thoughts you must have seen yourself living in a new place and pursuing a new passion," his iPhone told me as I shared my situation. "It must be true that everything happens first as a thought? Thought... something to think about... Have a wonderful day!"

I quickly got used to being asked again, after so many months alone, "How was your day?" BareChestMan had found my soft spot.

All of this, and we still hadn't met. Until this hot afternoon, when I stopped home after leaving my job of 15 years, picked up a bottle of chilled bubbly, and headed for Monarch Bay and a tee time.

BareChestMan was at the driving range, and we hugged and he whispered in my ear, "Just as cute as your pictures." He looked fine to me too — except, darn, we both got so sweaty walking 18 holes that day. BareChestMan had some game — wasn't wild and unmannered like BondMan — and made for great company. Except, darn... oh, I mentioned we both got so sweaty. And there wasn't, I sensed, that mythical-to-me instant chemistry.

I told him I'd had my share of disastrous golf dates, and that morning had thought about how I'd want to spend the evening after this one. So back at my new, hardly furnished apartment, I had left marinating a fresh tomato sauce with chopped heirlooms, garlic, basil, and olive oil. All it needed to become dinner was the uncorking of a bottle of wine and the cooking of a package of linguine.

"What's she trying to tell me?" he surely wondered.

When we walked off the 18th green at sunset, my head starting to pound from the heat and the Champagne, I invited BareChestMan to be my first dinner guest in my new place. Wow, was he surprised — probably wondering, is she so trusting of everyone? But he accepted, and we had a lovely evening watching a blazing sunset on the patio before he kissed me goodnight on the cheek.

"Thank you for one of the nicest days I have ever had," he texted later.

And we never saw each other again.

I would have liked to have gotten to know BareChestMan a bit better, but he went to see his family in Hawaii a few days later and did not text me or email when he returned. He maybe was hoping for some magic that he did not find with me. Whatever, I did not need an explanation — as well-practiced as I had become after now 15 such encounters, having one lovely first date and no others without commentary seemed a fine result, much better than many others.

No. 16, about a week later, I met for a little putting practice at his local course. My date was a great-looking guy a little bit older than me who wanted to give me putting tips. Then we had a little contest and I, apparently forgetting everything I had learned in eight months of dating, won. The next day, I emailed to fib, alas, I had some unfinished business with a previous fish in the sea and I wished him well.

Over the weekend, I thought about the effort I had made over the course of the year to connect with someone. Not to find a husband, a boyfriend, a lover — just to connect with someone who might in time fit one of those descriptions. Who might play golf with me, giggle with me, keep my feet warm at night. Who would look at me and see who I was, yet still want to look some more.

I looked in the mirror and didn't want a makeover or a facelift. I saw someone who had been honest and tried to be kind, even while charged with protecting her overly trusting and optimistic bleeding Frida heart.

I remember my friend Kristin telling me it had taken her something like 15 different dates to meet her match. I had had 16. Maybe it was time to take a break, I thought.

But just before I checked out of PlentyOfFish.com, there was unfinished business with RedTeeMan, who had winked at me months before on Match.com and now had gotten my attention.

His profile said:

> **I consider myself a realist but try to see the glass as "half full." I believe in a healthy body, mind and soul. Family and friends are important to me. I have all the educational degrees and work hard at my job. I work out 5-6 days a week, love movies, live jazz, fine dining, the theater, and being with friends. I'm a news and sports junky and manage my own investments. Please no drama!**

I thought maybe he was too old for me, and too serious. I envisioned a man whose nose was buried in the newspaper each morning as he studied the stock market reports over his coffee. I hadn't returned his wink months earlier. Instead, I had put him in my "maybe" basket.

Now his note said:

> **Hi, I liked your profile and photos and would like to meet you. Hope you review my profile and decide to contact me. Have a good holiday weekend.**

Deep breath.

Hi, I'm Susan, your profile is short and sweet! (also beautiful eyes and I see a hint of dimples...) ... Where are you in Oakland? I recently moved downtown, it is quite happening and I just love it. Also I recently left my career to regroup and work on starting my own business, so I am taking the next two to three months off to just relax and enjoy the Bay Area, friends, family, etc. I have been working fairly nonstop since I was 21 so it is a treat. Life is short, yada yada yada.

Hi Susan. I relocated from Laguna Beach for a new job. I'm VP of Marketing for an Internet startup. I just got an apartment not far from you while I look for a house. We're neighbors! If you have time give me a call ...

He said he liked golf, and suggested some possible outings we might have someday. And then on September 10:

Hi Susan, would you like to meet for a drink around 6 tomorrow afternoon on the waterfront?

Honestly, I was so tired of meet-and-greets and so unexcited about yet another that if I had had to do anything more than take a little two-block stroll to meet RedTeeMan, I would not have gone.

But my mind's answer to "What is the point?" was "What is the harm?" and on September 11 I dragged myself away from the pool to shower and put on a dress and trudge to my next date as if he were an uphill, 800-yard par-5.

CHAPTER SEVENTEEN

RedTeeMan

He was late, it was crowded, and I was just about to order a cocktail when there he was, looking pretty crisp in his blue blazer and white shirt. (The cuffs, I'd notice later, were monogrammed. Whew!)

Crisp, but a bit shiny and frazzled. Powerfully built, but definitely not as tall as the 6 feet he advertised. Still, I reached for his hand and we gave each other a peck. "I just flew in from a meeting in Chicago," he said. "I'm so sorry I'm late."

We got a table alongside the Bay, and, as he talked, the woman who had trudged rather forlornly along the street to the meeting place began to sit up straighter and straighter and straighter.

One thing he wanted to clear up right away: he was actually a year older than his listing, having made a mistake he was unable to change. Out came his license (57, not 56), to prove it.

Otherwise, Ivy League. MBA, and then a career in sales and entrepreneurship, including a company he had founded. This new company — which he had, he said, co-founded with some other super-smart guys — sold communications systems to mega-companies, and he gave me his pitch.

"Where do I sign?" I said laughing, as he pushed an imaginary contract and pen toward me and said, "Right here."

He loved money, he said. He did not care for petite women, he said, but preferred women like me with breasts and hips and curves. He had little to say to younger women, he said, and his most recent girlfriend had been five years older than him and a couple of inches taller.

When I said it was something of a red flag that a man his age had never been married — and, he added, never even lived with a woman — he was quick to the defense.

"Well maybe that's not because I was the one who didn't want to get married."

"Really?" I said, surprised, then asking matter-of-factly, "Any issue with monogamy or commitment?"

He shook his head no with an "I don't get it" sort of shrug. Then he told a heart-wrenching story about an early love, a shopkeeper he had pursued and to whom he had proposed. "I went on my first business trip," he said, "and I thought I did all the right things, called every day. I came home and she picked me up at the airport and started crying. She was wearing a wedding ring."

While he was gone, he told me, she'd married the recently single friend of his who had been joining them for their company many evenings.

But he was engaged other times, he said, and there were other stories about rejection suffered. The most recent, five-years-older fiancée, he said, had given him an ultimatum to move to her city or it was over. He didn't, he said, do ultimatums.

He told me about a one-nighter with an actress that had produced a daughter he had learned about later when he received a court summons. The actress had died tragically just a few years ago, he said, and their young, divorced daughter now had two children he was having to greatly support.

He'd moved back to the Bay Area, he said, to be closer to his aging parents and the rest of his family, so he was looking for a house in the Oakland hills. He traveled a lot, he said, and he would be leaving next for Las Vegas, which he said he often visited but seldom enjoyed.

I told him I didn't care if I got married again but wanted a partner, and he said he still hoped to get married someday. I answered some of his questions about my marriage but said it wasn't something I liked to talk about until I got to know someone better. He seemed more interested, anyway, in my golf outings with Frank and the editors, and I had one coming up the next morning.

Unlike some of my previous dates whose eyes had gone vacant when they heard I was willingly, enthusiastically leaving my job of 15 years, he lit up. I told him I wanted to start my own business, and he joked that when I made my first million there was a new Rolls Royce he would like to have called the Ghost.

Suddenly I realized it was after nine, and we had just planned to have drinks. I jumped up as if I had somewhere to go. He picked up the check and I said I would reciprocate some other time.

"That means there'll be another time?" he asked.

"I'd love to!"

I meant it. We embraced and I headed home with all the bounce that had been missing from my step three hours earlier. My heart pounded and I think I was even sweating. Finally, a man I could talk to who I didn't at all mind looking at, who made me laugh and laughed at my jokes and seemed so compatible! And even seemed to want a relationship and maybe even be ready for one! All these dates and finally it seemed okay for me to feel excited about someone.

I knew by now that I was supposed to wait for him to follow up. I didn't wait even 24 hours to email.

Hi, hope you had a good day? I guess I got so caught up in the conversation last night, I forgot you were hungry, and the time went by so fast. Did you find a sandwich someplace? I usually have no trouble falling asleep but last night I think I was a little too excited! Phew. We are different but I kinda see some poetry in the differences. Nice. Did you get to see any of the lightning show later? I do miss those so it was a treat. I would love to plan another outing when you have an evening

free, or maybe even a little twilight golf. Enjoy Vegas.

He called on Sunday to see if I would like to join him at an art-and-wine fair, but I was playing golf with my gal pals. That night he went off to Vegas.

"I'll be home at 10:30 tonight," he texted me on Wednesday.

Uh, did he expect to see me when he got home? I was usually in bed watching the news and starting to doze off by then, not heading out on the town.

"How about dinner Thursday night?" I asked.

So we had our first real date and now I could finally get excited, so excited that my dating advisory board felt it necessary to give me a no-sex-on-the-first-date edict. I agreed — but never had to rebuff an overture. Something seemed to happen in the course of the evening of dinner at my favorite local spot followed by drinks on a bayside patio. He seemed to drift away at some point, and when he walked me home and did not kiss me goodnight but sort of shook my hand, I immediately went upstairs and fired up my laptop.

So I had a really nice time, did I say or do something that made you uncomfortable? Had this feeling like the Southwest Airlines commercials, you wanted to get away -- just wondering.

At the very least, I figured, I would learn something from this failure. I couldn't keep shanking the ball without getting a lesson. I went to bed. In the morning I saw that he had replied 19 minutes later.

I got the feeling I was too forward with you and you put me back in 'check' twice tonight. I wanted to ensure you didn't feel any pressure. I too enjoyed your company but got the feeling you were uncomfortable every time I tried to touch you. It surprised me when you said there was 'no chemistry' when you first saw and met me because I had that for you. Maybe this will be a 'friends' thing.

I had never said there was no chemistry. I certainly did not rebuff any touch. Had he expected me to gush and fawn in some way I didn't? Or was he just a terribly sensitive man, not at all as tough as he appeared?

I partly blamed my advisory board for putting me at arm's length in a figurative sense that he perceived literally. But we obviously had a misunderstanding. A 180-degree misunderstanding.

So I wrote back:

Phew, dating is difficult not just for the guys!

First of all, you must have misheard on the chemistry. I kinda hate that word and don't use it, and what I was trying to say was that when we met for drinks I was just so discouraged by the whole process that I almost missed a good thing! Really as we sat there and talked that night you just blew me away. I couldn't wait to see you again. I haven't felt that way after any of dates 1 through 16 or really anyone.

My main goal last night was to have a proper dinner date, get to know you better and vice versa. Was trying to keep myself in check. Oops! Did not mean for that to

be contagious in any way. Isn't that funny?

So there you have it. I think I'm a little too attracted to you for a friends thing, but will keep an open mind about that. Hope you will want to spend more time together.

We did spend a lot more time together and soon he was calling me just about every day. We clicked. I had no trouble letting him take the lead on the phone calls because he was so busy with work and I did not want to bother him; he let me plan fun dates that he'd almost always pay for, and we saw each other just about every Saturday night and usually a couple of more times during the week.

It wasn't unusual for him to stop by in the middle of his day of appointments to sit on my couch and read the paper, or take me to lunch. I loved talking news and business and politics with him and we liked to watch the nightly news together. In fact, we could be spending more time together, he told me, if I wasn't such an early fader and he could come by after late racquetball matches and business dinners. If he arrived at a reasonably early hour, even before 10, I would stay up until midnight. But one night we tried to meet after my self-imposed 10 p.m. weeknight curfew because a series of business dinners had come between us, and I dozed off and apparently slept through the doorbell. He tortured me frequently with his account of his humiliation as the security guard downstairs watched him buzzing away in futility.

When I made a press trip to Kauai, he called me every

day and finally told me that was just the sort of thing he was free to go and do — as long as he had a phone and Internet, he said, he could work from anywhere.

"Great!" I said. "There'll be other trips."

I mentioned I'd like to go to Las Vegas and he told me, "You can come with me next time I go."

I was working on a freelance piece that fall related to the Pebble Beach golf tournament and had to go down to the Monterey Peninsula for a few days, but he had to travel to Chicago and could not join me, he said. This was not an easy trip, because it had been such a special destination for me and Marc. I had gone back to Tahoe and even to Plumas, where we had so many times vacationed. But, Pebble Beach and the Monterey Peninsula are special in any annals of golf and would not submit so easily to "That was then and this is now."

I tried playing golf after my first long morning of interviews, in fact, and my swing mysteriously disappeared. Nothing worked, not my chipping or putting — I was so out of sorts and lonely being there without Marc, who seemed to belong there with me. I even considered skipping a tee-time the women at the tournament offices had kindly arranged for me at Poppy Hills on the last day of my visit.

Me, the golf slut, skipping golf?

"Go," they said when I awkwardly explained my reluctance in the wake of our divorce. "You'll feel better."

I finally called RedTeeMan for a chat, and he said, "Why haven't you called me back?"

I didn't know I had gotten any messages from him. Indeed, I had not gotten these messages and never would — they vanished into 3G-land or found their way onto someone else's voice-mail. But he said he had called and left a message that his plans had changed and he wanted to come down and play golf with me.

"Oh, darn, I wish I had known," I said, thinking that would have certainly cheered me up. "Well then, I'll see you when I get home."

I got home late that night because, yes, I played Poppy Hills. While on the front nine, as I continued to look fruitlessly for my golf swing and my game, I started to think about all the amazing places I had visited with Marc and to accept that that part of my life was over and now I had a new life and the opportunity for a relationship with someone who made me feel safe.

On the back nine at Poppy Hills, playing at twilight with strangers, my golf swing started to return as my grief over the past gave way to hope.

I felt so safe and at ease with RedTeeMan, who seemed to make a very good living, avoided all drugs and rarely had more than one glass of wine when we were together. Of course he had his foibles — he took several showers a day, seemed rather socially awkward when it came to my friends, and had an addiction to working out that probably was related to his vanity. In fact when he got off a plane it was not me he wanted to visit, it was the gym. He changed his sheets every day, or so he told me — with the exception of one brief "here's where I live" tour of his apartment, we always were at my place. (When I remarked on this a few times, he said that he had nothing in his fridge and my place felt more like a home than his. Dealing with a lifelong bachelor, I did not doubt the truth of either point.)

He seemed to work all of the time, and had never taken a real vacation — any trips we would take together would be related to my business, it turned out. He traveled more than anyone I had ever known (look, I hadn't dated any near-C-level executives or even, until now, known that that meant the CEO type), and his friends told him the George Clooney character in *Up in the Air* appeared to have been based on him (he said he didn't see that at all). Most alien of all to me, he traveled for work even on weekends — because, he said, that's when engineers worked and would have the time to demo his product.

He hardly ever played golf with me because, he said I would learn when I founded a company of my own, his business demanded too much of his time. Even when he was home, it seemed his calendar invariably alerted him for a bike race or a tennis match, not golf with Susan.

I named him RedTeeMan here because on our rare golf outings he would come up to the forward tees and play from wherever I'd play.

At first I'd think, maybe I should move back so that he could play from the tees that suited his game better. His toned, powerful body, even with two artificial hips, a piece of steel in his back from a motorcycle accident, and a scar on his thigh where he said he had been stabbed protecting his wallet from a mugger, gave him plenty of strength and he could hit the ball a long way. That meant trouble playing from tees that are too short, because beyond the typical landing area the fairways would narrow and obstacles would loom.

But he told me (and whichever curious folk paired up with us), "We don't get to spend much time together because I'm traveling so much. I'd rather come up here and hit with you than go back there and tee off by myself."

Once when we played with a couple older than us, the other man decided that sounded like fun, and all four of us played the forward tees. This was even before the PGA of America created its "Tee It Forward" initiative, encouraging golfers to move up a tee or two because they would have more fun, lose fewer golf balls, and move along faster.

Theoretically, anyway.

The truth is, most men are so fixated on how far they think they should hit the ball that they cannot adjust to how far they actually hit the ball.

On one fam trip, a vendor had a party in his offices, and invited each of us to take three shots on a simulation of the famous seventh hole at Pebble Beach. The hole measures less than 100 yards from all but the very back tees, but the tee box is perched high over the green, unprotected along the edge of the ocean and demanding of some serious meteorological analysis. I watched some of the guests before me take their cuts and noticed they were all coming up short — maybe the fake wind was blowing in. I decided to give it a try, too, even teetering in heels and protecting my cleavage, and even with only stiff clubs designed for strong men players. When my nine-iron came up short, I put it back and tried an eight-iron. And when that came up short, I put it back and tried a seven-iron, which I would usually hit 115 yards or so. My hole-high shot settled about 12 feet right of the hole — and on top of the virtual leaderboard!

Then I settled on the couch and watch man after man pick out a club and stick with that same club even after shot one and then shot two landed short of the green on the screen. Our host was so tickled when I prevailed, he went to the storeroom and brought me back an armful of logo merchandise. I could not gloat, however, because I knew that I had not demonstrated superior skills; quite to the contrary. I demonstrated only that delusions of grandeur would not stand between me and a club change. (Besides, the merchandise was all made and sized for men.)

RedTeeMan would not have let his pride stop him from winning; he'd hit driver on a par-3 if he thought that's what he had to do to make a hole-in-one. He attached no yardage numbers to his clubs and if anything the ball usually flew much farther than he expected. Maybe he just didn't play enough golf to fall into the usual testosterone traps.

RedTeeMan typically seemed flustered and impatient at the beginning of the round, checking his phone for messages and attending to last-minute business. Then he'd gradually relax and become interested in improving his game. Others seemed to enjoy his company on the course because he had such a gentle, quiet manner about him; he fit in even at my publisher's country club, which I don't think had any black members. I had neglected to give a heads-up about RedTeeMan's race because I never thought about it. As we pulled into the parking lot, I swear I saw Frank's wife chuckling in bemusement. Frank never blinked and hosted us graciously.

RedTeeMan hit such amazing shots that day, I accused him of practicing behind my back. He rolled his eyes. "Yes, that's what I do when I leave your place after the 11 o'clock news," he said. "I go to the driving range and practice." We hadn't played together in weeks, and he looked far more competent than rusty. One shot flew out of such an unmanageable predicament and landed so close to the pin that I, not paying much attention, thought he must have improved his lie. Frank routinely did a thing men describe as "rolling the ball," where he would simply use his club to maneuver the ball into a more hittable lie, so a little bump in a bad place would not have violated the spirit of this afternoon. But this predicament would have required a big bump for relief — not to mention an admission of guilt when everyone was raving about the shot. RedTeeMan, however, shrugged off the oohs and aahs as if he expected to make the PGA Tour next fall.

Sometimes we would have a friendly but competitive

match and RedTeeMan would play better than me, but I noticed that he began to lose interest after 12 or 13 holes and I could usually come back and make it close. We talked about a life where we could play more golf and he could become really good at the game, which I did not doubt he could. I liked the idea — and I did not think it was a coincidence that when I dug those Nike golf shoes out of the back of my closet, they fit him.

We had been seeing each other only a couple of months when he announced that he was giving me a plane ticket home to Baltimore for Thanksgiving as my Christmas present. He said he could not be with me because this holiday in particular was always a big family occasion with birthdays and such attached. I thought, okay, he doesn't feel ready yet to include me so this is a nice gesture so I won't be alone.

But I noticed his online dating profile was still up and running and active, at both Plenty of Fish and Match. I had taken my own profiles out of view, but had access and anyone could see when he was "active within the last hour" and sometimes "online now." Rather than freak out about it, I talked to him.

"It seems like things are going really well with us," I said. "So I'm wondering why you are still on these sites representing yourself as available and looking for someone."

He seemed taken aback, and said that he believed there's a process that cannot be rushed, and that for him maybe the process takes a little longer, and that things were going well and he wanted to make sure I was over my marriage. In fact, he said, he did not even know if I was divorced yet, a somewhat significant fact I was sure I had shared.

So now the conversation turned to my readiness for a relationship. I had been divorced since July and Marc and I weren't even talking anymore because he was angry at how my employer had handled the benefits in the end. What especially irked Marc, oddly, was the revocation of his coverage under my health insurance policy. Despite my suggestions that he get checked out, he had not gone to see a doctor in the entire time I had known him — with the exception of one fainting incident at the golf course that left him with a gash on his nose that required stitches at an emergency care center. Yet he was furious at how quickly my company ceased his coverage while taking forever to disperse the payout he had elected to take rather than wait for a portion of my pension. I thought sometimes of calling to see how he was doing, but honestly did not want to extend myself when it was likely Marc would take advantage of the opportunity to vent rage and frustration at me.

But, wait, hadn't I intended this little talk to be about my current relationship? RedTeeMan expertly practiced "the best defense is a good offense," a true-to-life sports maxim dictating that one under siege ought to fire away. When he went on a trip around Easter and disappeared from phone and text for several days, I was irritated when I finally heard from him and we had a snippy conversation that ended with him saying something like, "I'm out here working hard when I would rather be there and I finally find the time to call and this is what I get?"

I started to apologize, when I realized he had done it again, reversing the charges so to speak. So when we talked later I took notes on what he had to say: "I try to bring comfort and joy into my relationships, and if that's not happening then it's time to reevaluate things. It has been a hectic, hellish trip, and I'm not the most sensitive, thoughtful person you'll ever know but I try and I am sorry if that's not enough. If you are having continual hurt feelings, which it sounds like you are, then come Sunday when I come home, let's be frank and make some decisions."

On the back of the piece of paper, I noted "he's not apologizing for not keeping in touch and connected, he's apologizing for my hurt feelings." I wondered, was I too demanding? Expecting too much of someone who had not been married and perhaps did not know how to connect two lives? There were often sweet "I miss you" cards and postcards coming from his travels. There was always a different gift basket of some kind (always from the same company), for holidays and special occasions. Christmas Eve had been absolutely beautiful, with fun gifts exchanged and a lovely dinner at my place, and though I was disappointed we could not spend New Year's Eve together I understood he had committed to watching his grandkids for the night. I wanted to join him for that but settled for a few phone calls during the evening instead, tickled when he put the toddlers on the line to say hello to Susan.

Together we had been following the biggest story in sports that fall, the Tiger Woods sex scandal. While we were spending Thanksgiving with our respective families, golf's superstar was being whisked off to the hospital to get attention for injuries sustained in what turned out to be an argument with his wife, who had been enraged by a tabloid story detailing one of his affairs. In the weeks to come, at least six more women would confess to extramarital liaisons — some in great detail, including transcripts of racy text messages that added the term "sexting" to the cultural lexicon.

RedTeeMan marveled at how such a phenomenal talent could make the time and maintain the secrecy required by such exploits, but if he was secretly envious and thinking, well, who wouldn't have seven affairs if he could get away with it, he never let on.

In fact, he was beginning to use the word "we" referring not to his business but to us. Increasingly, he would take me with him on his weekend house-hunting expeditions. When he said he was most interested in the investment prospects of a house, and less interested in its various features, I pointed out that if things continued to go well for us I might be living in that house with him. Not meaning to sound presumptuous but positive, I advised him, "I'm just saying, I don't think you want to buy a house that I hate." He laughed and later told me he had given his agent this new criterion.

When he had to make a business trip to Japan that summer, our relationship seemed to deepen. He texted or called several times every day, and when he came home he brought gifts (including a golf GPS that would give me my yardage to the hole from anywhere on the course, yay!) and gave me a very romantic card that brought tears to my eyes.

His profile was still alive and kicking on the dating sites, but he always seemed to be available when I needed him and honored every commitment he made to me. Best of all, he was coaching me on a plan for my new business. I decided to focus on my career goals for now, and when I felt I needed RedTeeMan to step it up, I would just ask him to and be prepared for the consequences.

CHAPTER EIGHTEEN

GottaGoGolf

I n 2008, *Golf For Women* magazine abruptly shut down. It had a subscriber base of 600,000 and seemed to be supported by ads, but its big parent company, Conde Nast, deemed it unworthy of sustaining in a print-hostile era and dismal economy.

I quickly emailed my women friends in the golf industry, Cori and Emmy, and proposed we step up to replace it. Right now.

"It had gotten too elitist anyway, with all the celebrities and thousand-dollar shoes," I pitched them. "Let's get in there and fill the void with something more fun, something for all of the women who play golf, not just the country club set."

They both demurred. Neither was interested in making such a career commitment.

So I had kept working at the paper. Now that I wasn't, I started working on a plan to start my own magazine, a cross between *Golf Digest* and *Oprah* that I would title *Golf Goddess*.

My magazine, I decided, would be all-digital, because that would be the way we would all be reading magazines in five to 10 years. And I wouldn't give it away, the way my company had so misguidedly given away my work on the Internet all those years.

And, there would be no tips and lessons! The golf magazines do all of that, ad nauseum. So do the books and videos. I, golf slut and bogey golfer, could not hope to improve on expert content. But what I could do was advocate for women, and present content with a sassy voice that speaks to them. My magazine would review courses, destinations and equipment for the average woman golfer, not the avid male golfer the other golf publications fought over. It would keep in mind that perhaps 20 percent of women golfers are gay, or at least maybe not skort wearers, and that a good chunk of the rest play golf with their husbands.

I will not begin to list the mistakes I made. Because I might never finish.

But RedTeeMan helped me create a modest PowerPoint and supplemental materials that represented my analysis of the market and my concept of the product. He regularly brought me envelopes full of clippings he thought relevant to my endeavor, and would call to tell me of a business-related TV program he'd just seen that I ought to record.

He taught me the meaning of ROI — the venture capitalist's holy grail, return on investment. He asked me, "What's your value proposition?" He helped me list my differentiators.

I went to Small Business Administration workshops, and saw a consultant there. I found seminars on search engine optimization and social media, and learned all I could about the digital publishing medium. I met with my golf buddy Frank, who tossed an idea or two my way later that made me some money.

I saw clearly what I could do well — oversee the project, set and hit deadlines, write and edit, do PR and marketing. My original golf partner friend Cheryl wanted to work on the web part of the project, so I needed a design partner and a business/sales person.

And, in the great network of contacts with which I left the newspaper, I found a couple of energetic supporters who could fill those voids. It's just that, after six months or so, nothing was really happening. I was expecting everyone to own their areas and report back to me with ideas and plans, and maybe they were expecting me to order them around.

And then in June 2010 I went on the annual Golf the High Sierra Media Tour. (Again, I am not sure why I was invited, not having any job at the time.) And there on the first tee of Genoa Lakes I met Lynn DeBruin.

Lynn rushed up and jumped into in my cart, splaying her camera and notebook and a whole bag of accessories onto the floor and into compartments. She was late because she had stopped at the other Genoa Lakes course by mistake and, being from Colorado and all, didn't know any better.

I took a big breath, and continued to do so during my

time with Lynn. A cancer survivor who had been laid off by her newspaper, she lived fast, talked fast, ran late, and misplaced things even within the narrow boundaries of the golf cart. My former "detach" mantra made us the perfect golf partners. At one course, we were pitted against the boys in a match and when we weren't doing very well went into the ladies room at the turn together.

"My bra is pinching me, I'm taking it off," I announced.

"My panties are chafing, I'm taking them off," she said from the next stall.

We kicked ass on the back nine.

Lynn listened to my plan for my magazine and said, "Why don't you do it?" And then as the week went on, she said, "I think you must do it." And then after she went home, she called to say, "Get going on this!"

Lynn made a list of content she could contribute, and then she got it done. She called me with ideas and contacts, she kept after me, and so, I really had to do it.

My design partner said later that she didn't believe we were really going to get it done and she credited me for pushing for it. But I think it was Lynn who was behind it all. She then got a perfectly normal job and exited the project, only to have the cancer come back and end her life at 51. For me, it was as if she was this little angel who showed up at the right time to make this one little miracle.

It was a miracle, really, produced on time on October 1, 2010 — a prototype issue of *GottaGoGolf. Golf Goddess* had some trademark issues that would have kept us from expanding the brand, and anyway I had decided, why should I have an "ess," a "her," a "woman" or "lady" or "ette" in the title of my magazine for women who play the game for fun? *Golf Digest* didn't need to tell readers it was for men, it just so obviously and clearly was.

My designer made *GottaGoGolf* gorgeously for women and I made it interestingly for women, and we made something of a splash in the golf industry.

On my way home from the last push at my designer's house, tired but triumphant, I called RedTeeMan to tell him *GottaGoGolf* was online and ready for readers. I wanted to thank him for all his encouragement and wisdom.

It was after midnight on a Friday night, and he didn't answer or call back.

We had been seeing each other for more than a year. He was, I would tell people, "the man in my life." I couldn't quite go the route of Jackson Browne, who, noting that he was well past the time to have girlfriends, referred to the woman in his life as "My Stunning Mystery Companion." Once when we were sitting stage-side at a comedy show, the comedian asked, "Who here is in a relationship?" RedTeeMan raised his hand and I asked, "Who is she?" A joke, sort of, but then...

I still hadn't met his daughter or grandchildren. I had met his parents finally but that wasn't his idea but something he arranged to appease me. I had not met any colleagues, and only one friend, a woman, who happened to be in town visiting the wine country. And now that my magazine was a thing, I looked on Match.com, just curious, and there he was, still looking for love.

I pretended the two of us were in a relationship together and asked him how he would like to spend the holidays this year. He looked confused, clearly not having given any thought to including me in his plans, and said, "You know this is a big family occasion for me." I was on the outside of his life, and so I did not invite him into my inner circle for a family trip that month to South Carolina. And in fact, I decided that if he wanted to spend the rest of his life on Match.com, I was okay with that and ready to move on. I loved him, but by now I felt that he either couldn't or wouldn't be a partner to me. And it didn't matter whether he couldn't or wouldn't, it just wasn't.

So in what I thought was a very upbeat, positive, caring conversation over dinner, I told him I saw he was still on Match.com even though things seemed to be going so well for us. In between bites on a crab sandwich, I asked him to take some time while I was traveling and decide if he wanted to be all in or if we should move on.

For once, he did not attack. In fact, he seemed utterly crushed. He put down his fork, and his head hung. "I haven't slept with anyone else since we met," he told me, which struck me as an odd thing to say considering that I hadn't accused him of anything along those lines. "It seems to me that you don't believe in us."

He never finished his food, and when he dropped me off at home he did not come in.

I stayed upbeat. It wasn't my mission in life to nag a man, and here again, I wasn't going to give any ultimatums or make any demands.

"You know, chances are that if I'm on Match.com trying to meet Joe and flirt with Jim, I'm not focused on what I need to do to be a good partner to you," I told him. "Relationships are hard. I am sure you can always find someone prettier or smarter or richer than me, and if that's what you want, you should go for it. And I should find someone who wants to be a partner to me."

"Relationships are hard," he agreed.

The next morning as I sat on the plane waiting to take off, I fired off a quick email to him.

I would never take a trip like this without telling you I love you and will miss you.

As for the rest, if I did not believe in us I would have slinked away by now. Every issue I raise is a sign of my commitment to create a true and honest partnership. Conflict is inevitable, how will we resolve them? Is it you vs. me or is it you and me vs. the challenges of two independent adults coming together? Will you turn to me and work with me or will you turn away and retreat in anger? Can we find ways to negotiate and fight fair so we both feel heard? All important questions for us to examine and answer, too important to evade. I personally would like us to do much better.

Within an hour, he replied.

You made good points and I agree about partnership, conflict being inevitable, etc. What concerns me is I thought I answered your question directly and honestly. You got upset because you didn't think I answered it. There's a big gap there. Second, you seem to be more and more unhappy with things - or maybe you're just speaking out more. These are the points that have me concerned.

I didn't know what question he meant. But I sent along family pictures from the gathering, a golf-less celebration in golf-rich Hilton Head, in honor of my brother's 20 years of sobriety. And a couple of times I called. He sent one stiff email with a couple of business contacts in it that said:

I think about you several times a day and what's been happening these last couple of weeks. Hope you're enjoying your vacation.

But my calls to RedTeeMan went unanswered, and by the time I heard the whir of the landing gears over Oakland, I realized I had to accept that he was answering me with his silence.

I kept looking at my phone for the blink of an email or phone message. Day after day, nothing. My shock gave way to anger — how could he treat me so dismissively? Did I not deserve better?

Of course I did, my friends assured me. And so I raged and mourned and healed, preparing, as the saying goes, to "get back out there." Back on Match.com, I started corresponding with a man who was coming out of his third marriage and didn't want to rush into his next big thing. "It's important to me to be friends first," he said.

There was one thing I had to do, of course, before I could move on. I had to let RedTeeMan know how much he had hurt me, and how little respect I had for his exit strategy.

So a month after I had come home, on a Saturday morning when his phone would surely be in a locker at the gym, I left a voice-mail.

"Of course it occurred to me that things would not work out between us, but I always thought there would be a conversation, that we would wish each other well. Never would I have expected you to just, poof, disappear. I thought you were a grownup, that we would be kind to each other. I am moving on, I accept, but I need you to know how much that hurt me. I did not deserve that, and I am sure I will never understand it."

Then I took advantage of a neat smart-phone feature, tapping into RedTeeMan's profile, where I had given him his own unique ring tone, and selecting "Send to voice-mail."

So I would never hear his ringtone again. Which is good, because I would have heard it almost immediately, delivering an angry voice-mail on the attack: it was I who hadn't emailed or called, not him. "I figured you just got tired of my act," he said, giving me pause for a moment to wonder just what act he meant.

Once his anger passed, though, he turned to email and even handwritten notes to tell me how much he missed me. "Let's meet and talk face to face," he asked.

Maybe it was just another miscommunication, but I remembered those earlier missed connections and decided someone was trying to tell me something. I was no more a part of his life than when we had met, and I could not envision a life spent on the outside of RedTeeMan's circle trying and hoping to get inside.

FriendsFirst and I had a great, friends-first kind of date in Oakland and even went to brunch the next day. He emailed a few days later to say it seemed to him I was not "enough into" him.

So much for "friends first." I threw up my hands. Obviously I was not "enough" something or other, though I seemed plenty clueless when it came to men. Time for a break.

CHAPTER NINETEEN

Not Golf

"**I**'ve been so busy on this trip, from 8 a.m. until after dinner every day," I told my hostess at the Westin Ka'anapali. "I haven't even been to the beach."

"You mean," she said, eyes widening, "you have not even stuck your toes into the warm, clear waters of the Pacific Ocean?"

That's how it goes on a fam trip, and this December visit to Maui covered three parts of the island, all of them golf destinations. Golf every day, plus meetings and lessons and drive time to the next destination. I believe I insulted one of my hostesses by asking if I could watch the Ravens play the Steelers on Sunday night. (C'mon, it was their biggest game of the season.)

That was my closest proximity to the beach, a hut full of TVs and umbrella drinks.

Look, I'm not complaining. I am just pointing out that the life of a golf slut, like the life of a beach bum, has its hardships and limitations. I hardly had time to unpack from that fam when I got home, because the next day I was off to Tucson to experience the Ritz Carlton at Dove Mountain, a divine place where I someday hope to sleep in and then nap alongside the pristine infinity pool. Instead, I had a schedule full of golf, spa, and meals. Just another invitation I could not refuse.

By now, word had gotten out about *GottaGoGolf*, and I had mapped out the editorial calendar for the year. I also had put together a media kit to pitch prospective sponsors. Women in the industry stepped up to offer encouragement, assistance, and advice, but not much money was coming my way.

In fact, not much money was coming the way of anyone in the golf industry. Rounds had declined by at least 25 percent since the Tiger Woods-inspired boom of the early 2000s, and fewer people could justify spending time and money at play. Courses were closing. Housing communities that had once considered golf courses essential for marketing were now wondering how to turn them into bike trails and soccer fields.

Yes, I know — and I chose this time to launch a golf magazine for women. And I continued to make mistakes.

Never mind. While hard at work on the first of *GottaGoGolf*'s 10 issues of 2011, a Skype message popped up on my screen. A San Francisco creative firm needed an editorial director for a project involving golf and thought I'd be perfect — could we talk?

The firm's principals told me about a startup that saw the current, barren golf field as ripe for cultivating with a new, hip, appealing game that could be played on existing golf courses. Suppose, for instance, each player was given a mulligan per hole? Or could toss the ball out of the sand? And could tee it up in the fairway? All of this, with high-performance equipment that performed in ways that made hackers look like pros.

Heavy hitters from the Bay Area were behind the project, they told me, and they needed a website up and running before the PGA Expo. That would be three weeks later, a week or so before the next *GottaGoGolf* was due out. But I was too intrigued not to give it a go.

I signed a nondisclosure agreement and went to meet the principals. And there was Pat Gallagher, who had been head of marketing and then president of the San Francisco Giants when I covered baseball. I also met his friend and sidekick for the "Alternative Golf Association," an inventor named Bob Zider. And Damien Eastwood, former head of legal for Sun Microsystems.

They had other investors, they told me, but just one other principal.

I had already guessed — it was Silicon Valley superstar Scott McNealy, the founder and former CEO of Sun Microsystems. McNealy had been named top executive golfer by *Golf Digest* a few years running, and frequently appeared in the Pebble Beach Pro-Am. About a year earlier, he had sold his company to Oracle founder Larry Ellison for $7.4

billion — but what's a dynamic, ruthless, golfing CEO type to do but look for a new venture?

Try Flogton — that's "not golf" spelled backward. The AGA formed as a sort of governing body to oversee the development of this Project Flogton, which it envisioned as a viral social media phenomenon that would have rules and policies (and, it hoped, a new name) developed by the community at large.

The idea was Zider's, the implementation Gallagher's, the legalities Eastwood's, and, I guessed, the money was McNealy's.

Except, the first thing I noticed was that these guys wanted money from the golf heavyweights, particularly the equipment companies and course operators. They wanted to find or, in Zider's case, invent new equipment — high-performing stuff beyond the specifications of golf's ruling body, the USGA — and incorporate new rules and formats, so that golfers would have more fun and nongolfers would want to try the game. And they wanted partners in the industry to kick money into the kitty.

I loved the irreverence of the concept, and could see its appeal for women, who just want to hit the ball farther and might be willing to break a few little rules to do so. It's absurd that recreational players are limited to the same equipment that the pros use, equipment that is designed to fit their super-fast swing speeds yet keep them from hitting the ball so far as to make golf courses in need of extension. The rest of us need equipment designed to fit our slow swing speeds while giving us as much distance as technology will generate. If this equipment existed, I would want it.

I could see how a disdain for dress codes might open golf to more young people — it was ridiculous to me that country clubs dictated how much leg and even arm a woman golfer could show, while the LPGA players on TV were hiking their skorts ever higher. (Zider told of how his teenage daughter had been admonished for her outfit at the driving range, never to return.)

And I could see how different rules sets could create different kinds of games that could be played on existing layouts, within the existing geography. Golf is so hard — maybe something like this would make it a little easier.

So in many ways, Flogton and the AGA were aligned with *GottaGoGolf* — though the fellows let me know loud and clear, women were not their intended market. They were after the 18 million or so recreational golfers who weren't playing very often, most of whom were male.

But I loved working for Gallagher, Zider, Eastwood, and McNealy, four very smart, successful guys who returned my calls, answered my emails, and showed respect for my expertise in media, writing, and editing. Knowing they were looking for other heavy hitters to join their cause, I even suggested someone else I thought might fit. "Is he an asshole?" Gallagher asked. "We've all had successful careers and worked with plenty of assholes, and our deal here is that we're not inviting any assholes into the group." I briefly re-considered my candidate and said, "Never mind."

I was on board with great enthusiasm, figuring that this was exactly the sort of experience that could educate me with lessons that I could apply to my own startup. Gallagher, who became my supervising partner, opened up his market-ing mind to me, and shortly before the big launch I whipped up a trial event at an Oakland municipal golf course where we shot videos of players trying out different formats and clubs. One of Zider's inventions, a funky wedge that plopped short shots onto the green, was christened by them for the grid lines across its face: "the waffle iron." We were encour-aged by the fun reactions, although there was at least one traditionalist in the group who was appalled by the idea of teeing the ball up in the fairway. "I would have no interest in playing golf this way, I like the game fine as it is," he said.

By launch day, January 27, 2011, flogton.com had been filled with my copy about the rules, equipment, and the key players. I had prepared a press release:

Silicon Valley heavy hitters launch Project Flogton — "a new brand of golf for the rest of us"

It went around many times among the fellows for revi-sions, becoming the central piece in a press kit that also in-cluded thumbnail bios and a statement from the "commissioner," McNealy. I had made a bunch of money for the many hours and words, and was given a retainer to con-tinue as press liaison over the coming months.

Gallagher made time to call me in California after the

standing-room-only press conference in Orlando. "It was huge," he said. "Golf is dying for new ideas. The reception was great." The guys' gimmick was to wear jeans, and point out that they'd be kicked off many golf courses in such attire. Then they ran through their PowerPoint and handed out their press kit. All the top golf publications wrote stories.

"Turning Golf Tradition On Its Head" (*New York Times*)

"The new testament of golf" (*Wall Street Journal*)

"Flogton rights the wrongs of real golf" (*Washington Post*)

Even *Asian Golf Monthly* blew up the story, taking all the words I had written and adding fun photos from a shoot I arranged with a former colleague to generate a cover feature.

But by this time, Eastwood had exited to work on another McNealy startup. And the golf industry, which had gotten a shot of adrenalin from the expectation that a billionaire was setting out to save it, began to wonder why the AGA was looking for money.

It was, I learned, Zider who had been the founder, creator, and funder of the AGA and what we called "Project Flogton." Years earlier, he had met with USGA disapproval and personal frustration trying to secure an okay for a forgiving putter he had invented. There was nothing odd in the look of the putter; it simply had a face that was built so that off-center putts did not lose distance drastically. Who makes off-center putts? Mostly, us amateurs with high handicaps, but the USGA had reservations about what would happen if professionals could wield such a stick. Zider went away fuming, and the Alternative Golf Association began to grow in his files.

Zider was certain that nonconforming equipment of which the USGA did not approve was hidden in someone's prototype closet, and that recreational players could be persuaded to use this illegal stuff if only the game were not called golf but something else. ("Flogton" had legs and remains in the media vocabulary, even though Gallagher and friends had considered it only a placeholder until a better name came along.) Marketing and selling that equipment, along with a new game, would bring in the money that could save the golf industry.

McNealy did not plan to do that himself.

An avid golfer with a wife and four sons who played with him, his innovative ideas manifested in rules that would speed up the game and technology that would appeal to young people. "No cell phones on the course" would give way to "Turn your cell phone on and download the course app now." I loved the idea that my golf club could be implanted with a chip that would tell me all about what kind of contact I had made, how far I had hit the ball, and where it went. I loved the fun-golf rules that outlawed practice swings and might require one throw per hole.

I can toss the ball out of a 10-feet-high bunker? Where do I sign up?

Hey, I am a golf slut, but I am not a golf purist. I often wished I could call Marc and tell him all about this crazy venture. Though we were estranged, he was still the person I wanted to talk golf with, and the old, happy Marc would surely have gotten a kick out of Flogton.

I didn't have anyone special in my life now, and good thing. *GottaGoGolf* hit the virtual newsstand March 1, and I continued to wear two hats that fit together well. My work with the AGA introduced me to heavyweights in the PGA of America, golf course owners' association, and other groups that also connected to me for my appeal to women golfers. And it subsidized my magazine.

Which, curiously, wasn't quickly gaining a following. For one thing, I did not start with any lengthy contact lists and had to build on word of mouth. (I tried buying a list for a couple of months, but, chalk that up to my list of mistakes.) In the month I had the most readers open *GottaGoGolf*, I had bought an ad in a golf fitness magazine — but, I noticed with disappointment, the readers did not come back the next month when I did not buy an ad. Another digital magazine for which I was writing columns as the "Golf Goddess" seemed to be having a similar experience: First, digital subscribers had to open the email announcing the issue; next, they had to open the issue itself. Also my magazine was not iPad-friendly at first, and that did not help matters. Tablets were new but quickly gaining steam, and readers wanted to read magazines on them rather than laptops and PCs.

Aside from the tricky technicalities, it was the no-Lorena era on the women's pro tour. The LPGA had never turned women's golf into a prime-time TV sport, but some of its players had done more than their part. Nancy Lopez took the stage with a smile in the first part of the golf-on-TV era, and later Annika Sorenstam stepped up. At first quiet and demure, Annika did not endear herself to fans and media. But when in 2003, at age 32, she decided to take on the men and play in Texas in a PGA tournament to which she had been invited, she energized the sport the way Billie Jean King did tennis. Sorenstam, who had already achieved Hall of Fame status in the women's game, let the cameras watch her brutal training regimen (push-ups with 50 pounds strapped on!) and shared with viewers her hopes. "I'm curious to see if I can compete," she said.

Sorenstam did not make the cut, she missed by a shot. But the way she handled the pressure hushed the whiners who cried "publicity stunt." The woman did not need publicity — she had tied the tour record with 11 wins in a season a year earlier, and had broken the hallowed 60 mark with a 59 the year before. She also accepted an invitation to play in the prime-time *Battle at Bighorn* with Karrie Webb, David Duval, and Tiger Woods in 2001. She could go out to dinner and count on being noticed. That she tested herself at the PGA's Colonial gave little girls permission to try with all their might, and inspired Michelle Wie to play in PGA tournaments a few years later.

When Annika retired in 2005, Lorena Ochoa was standing by to captivate viewers. She did not look as powerful as Annika did in her later years, yet Ochoa generated swing speed with impeccable technique. She also chatted up the maintenance crews in Spanish when she came to town, and galvanized girls' golf in Mexico. A journalist I met on a fam trip told me women simply did not play golf in Mexico before Lorena became a star, and now they accounted for as much as 30 percent of play, he said. Then at 28 — maybe not even at the top of her game yet — she quit the LPGA Tour. She said she wanted to start a family.

That was in 2008, and this time the LPGA had no one in the wings. It had a lot of great athletes, beautiful athletes, classy athletes. But it had no Nancy, no Annika, no Lorena. It certainly had no captivating American star, and many of its athletes were coming from Japan, Korea, Taiwan. *GottaGoGolf* put smiling Yani Tseng on its cover as the face of the future of the LPGA Tour in the spring of 2011, but she soon fell off the GPS.

The LPGA marketing team stepped up to promote its global tour via TV and Twitter. The tour had many faces, yet it had no face. When I surveyed readers about what they wanted to read, the LPGA did not make their wish list.

I still hadn't found a development partner who could work the advertising, sales, and revenue side of *GottaGoGolf*, and I just did not have time to do everything. But I did as much marketing and outreach as I could reasonably do while also doing much of the writing, all of the assigning, and most of the editing. Whenever I went to events and gatherings of women golfers, the feedback was, "Cool! This looks great!

How come I've never heard of it?"

So there I was, working hard and spending away my nest egg, when a neat guy connected with me on one of those dating websites I still kind of eyeballed. He had worked for more than 30 years at the same company, and was not entirely at liberty to say exactly what he did. A big sports fan who seemed to be great companionship material. Married before but no kids, just like me. We decided to meet late on a Saturday afternoon on a putting green in between our addresses, and the chemistry bubbled. I think I avoided a contest at this point and we just chatted and putted, and then we decided to have a margarita nearby.

Things were going well, and I had told him proudly about the business I had started, when he said, "But what are you doing for a living? I mean, you must work for someone. This is just a hobby, right?" He went on about the oversaturated Internet, and how websites like mine were "a dime a dozen." It shocked me. And insulted me. He must have seen that, because he said, "I'm just kidding."

"No, you're not," I said quietly.

I considered leaving at that very moment — that is how important *GottaGoGolf* had become, and that is how much I valued what I had accomplished, and that is how quickly it had become clear that someone who thought it important to work all his life for the same company would find it impossible to approve of my choices.

Instead, I stayed to the end and even paid my half of the bill. As soon as I got into the car, the mushy texts started to flow into my phone — I had no time to say, "You seem like a great guy but I do not think we are a match." The next morning, golfing with my Sharp Park gals, I told them about my disappointment with the way my date had disrespected my business. One of them pointed out that we often react from the perspective of our own choices, and that maybe if he had a bit of time he might check out my magazine and my website and find it impressive. Deep down, I rejected this theory. After all, even from my seat as a fearless entrepreneur, I had been prepared to admire his own 30-year inertia as evidence of commitment, not fearfulness. But I waited a few days to see if that would be the case. It wasn't, and I wrote the polite rejection note that had become all too familiar.

RedTeeMan, who had never been anything but supportive of my ambitions, must have sensed his opening. He had continued to text, to email, to call — and so I sought his counsel when I went to conferences, had him review my media kit to send to potential ad buyers, welcomed his introductions to people he thought could help me. He continued to flirt with me, effectively challenging me to give him another chance to beat me on the golf course. When we finally reunited that summer, I told him that I no longer had any illusions that he would open himself to an intimate committed relationship with anyone, but he could take this time to demonstrate otherwise — at least until I met someone who really wanted those things with me.

"Do you understand what I am saying?" I asked, fixing an

intent gaze on him.

He nodded once, fast, and then changed the subject. This time around when the holidays approached, I did not ask him his plans. I just booked a flight for one to Baltimore for Thanksgiving.

CHAPTER TWENTY

One Last Round

I would rather play golf alone than suffer through unpleasant company. Getting back together with RedTeeMan reminded me of what I had learned from marriage — that the most profound and heartbreaking loneliness strikes not when we are alone, but when we are with those we love yet still feel alone. Sometimes, when RedTeeMan went off on his excursions, I missed being married and having someone who cared about where I was and what I was doing. I'd get under the covers and wish someone was there to warm my cold feet. Sometimes even when he was there with me, I missed being married and having someone who cared about where I was and what I was doing.

But golf with unpleasant company generally yields a lesson. Maybe just to open up to someone who seems different, only to be reminded that we are really all the same and we all want the same things. Maybe just to remember we all have good days and bad days. I saw RedTeeMan struggling with his work and his family obligations, sometimes seeming so distant and other times seeming so content to be anywhere with me, anywhere at all. No one else had come into my life, so surely I had something here to learn. He continued to be dependably there for me when he was not working.

Unlike the first year of our romance, however, I wasn't making myself dependably there for him. In fact, I was playing with my golf club almost every Sunday, a day when I used to enjoy looking at houses or hitting practice balls with the man in my life. And that's why I was returning my father's phone call from Sharp Park on that Sunday morning when I learned that Marc was in a coma and would soon be gone.

I reversed my usual 31-and-a-half-mile Sunday morning drive, leaving the cool coast for warmer sunshine as I headed for the Bay Bridge, gulping down deep breaths behind the wheel and blinking out the tears so they'd fall and not blind me in the bright light. I thought of Marc all alone at the end of his life, and, yes, I had the grandiosity to think, this would not have happened if we were still together. I thought of how very angry he was at me the last time I talked to him, almost two years ago, so angry about the way my company had dropped him from the health insurance coverage that to my knowledge he had never used. I thought of how I still had been keeping a carton of photos I'd sorted for him out in plain sight in my apartment. I'd planned to drop it off at his place on one sunny day, after first calling so that he wouldn't be hurt by the surprise or angry if he should spot me at his front door. The carton had been sitting there a year and a half, collecting dust.

I remembered how he would never go to a doctor, even after the fainting incidents at the golf course and at my parents' place. And how he opted for money up front when we split up, rather than wait for a share of my pension when I turned 65. He would say sometimes, when we discussed pensions and Social Security, "I probably won't even be around to collect it." Could he have known somehow?

When I got home, I called the hospital to see if I could come and see Marc. I opened that carton and pulled out a favorite photo of Marc, still in his golf clothes and hat after a round at Bodega Bay, smiling with the sunset behind him. I would put it on the table next to his bed, so that the doctors and the nurses could see who he had been, this man they were now making comfortable for the end of his life.

Before I went into his room, the nurse on duty told me what to expect. Machines were breathing for Marc. His brain probably was not functioning. He would not be awake or talking to me.

She walked me in and gave me a box of Kleenex.

I was struck at first by the TV. It was off, but wasn't there a NASCAR race or golf tournament that he would have been watching?

Then I saw Marc's face, those beautiful eyes still open and turned toward the window so that they were filled with light, and I was overcome by a deep peace. Tubes led to his mouth and to his heart, but I could feel that he was no longer suffering the pain of life or the pain of dying. I have never been in a more peaceful place than that room, where I held Marc's hand and told him I would always love him and miss him.

I talked to him a bit, even made a few jokes about my cold feet. I told him I had always hoped to get a phone call from him someday when he was in a 12-step program. I told him that he was still my favorite golf companion, and I asked him to scout out the courses and pick out a good one, I'd be there soon enough.

Mostly, I told him I wished him peace. I told him I would be looking forward to that day when we could play golf together again. It was a short, final goodbye.

I asked the nurse on duty if I could have a phone call after his family had decided to let him go. I told her what a lovely person he had been, and she gave me a hug. The hospital did not have a chapel, so I found a chair in a waiting area and sat quietly for a bit. Then I got back behind the wheel and drove to our old house to see Alex, our then next-door neighbor who had found him.

The house was quiet, and the little boy next door who had often come over to play with us answered, not so little anymore. His mom and I cried together. Alex had been in Marc's neighborhood early in the week and had stopped by when he saw Marc's truck outside. No one answered the door. "I figured, maybe he's in the shower or maybe he just doesn't want to be disturbed," Alex said. "So I left."

A couple of days passed before Marc's landlord became alarmed at the tickets collecting on Marc's truck. This time, he and Alex went into the apartment and found Marc, unconscious. He was still breathing, but maybe just waiting not to die alone, because shortly after the paramedics arrived, his heart stopped. The hospital was keeping him technically alive only so that his family could say goodbye.

Alex was inconsolable about not having made more of an effort to reach Marc sooner. But anyone would have thought what he had thought, done what he had done.

He told me a bit about Marc's life since we had been apart. Soon after we separated, Marc had been arrested for drunk driving. But instead of getting help, he retreated — staying home in his cozy apartment to drink and get high rather than going to the golf course or even over to Alex's house. There was no woman in his life, and he seldom had any work. Once, his buddies at the golf course made a cute little video for him, urging him to come back out to play, but to no avail.

Marc had gone to a clinic about a month earlier about what Alex described as simply "that thing on his stomach" and had asked Alex to be his emergency contact. When the doctor called me two days after my visit to tell me Marc was gone, she speculated that the lesion or tumor on his stomach probably had been there a long time, and that it probably had ruptured internally and quickly attacked his organs while he was home alone with no one to see what was happening.

I had not known about any "thing" on Marc's stomach. Yet I remembered that during my final visit with him in the hospital, I had instinctively and tenderly placed a hand on his belly.

The cause of death was toxic shock.

I asked the doctor about his visit to the clinic and whether he had been diagnosed with anything, and she said they had gotten him into "the system" and he had upcoming appointments at the public hospital. He did not have any health insurance, and so he had to wait in the long line of people down on their luck in the recession. I wondered how many others were dying in the prime of life because of their ill financial health, and there was some anger in the calls I made to as many of Marc's friends as I could reach — anger at the health care system, anger at the weed, and, yes, even some anger at Marc.

Mostly I saw grief in the mirror at this sad ending to Marc's story, to our story. With each phone call, I had to somehow collect myself to endure another person's sorrow. And when I was satisfied that I had reached everyone I could, I posted that great Bodega Bay photo of Marc on my Facebook page, and wrote, "Marc, 48, died peacefully at Alameda Hospital this afternoon with his family by his side. He loved NASCAR, the NHL and golf, a good chardonnay (but not too chilled), CSI reruns, and lasagna. Old school music from the '70s would get him shaking his booty every time, and it's quite possible he knows every line Nicholson and De Niro ever uttered in a film. His favorite birthday: pizza (pepperoni, sausage, green pepper and mushroom)-beer (Heineken)-movie (gangsters!). He was the best Scrabble opponent I have ever had. And, how about that smile?" Some of my "friends" did not know who he was and said it seemed I had lost someone very special.

There was no service planned by Marc's family, however. And for me, for the friends who grieved, that would not do. Everyone deserves some sort of sendoff, some sort of tribute, some thank you for having been here, and so his friends and I pooled resources for a Perfect Marc Day in his honor.

Nine holes of golf at his home course, followed by pizza and beer at the restaurant of one of his golf pals. We made our way around the course with a few Heinekens talking about Marc, repeating many of his little sayings... "There's still some meat left on that bone" for when a putt did not get very close to the hole... "Run, Forrest, run," when a low-flying ball got rolling... "I didn't come here to lay up," when a pond or bunker stood between a player and the hole. Though it was December 1, the day was quite nice except for a mischievous little wind — a sign, I said, that Marc had some pull wherever he now was and had kept his sense of humor.

As we finished our round, a bagpiper showed up on the last hole and played a few songs, nothing too mournful because I remembered that the man I married had not liked sad music. Anyway, we all were sad enough.

The upstairs room at the pizza place slowly filled with golf friends, ex-neighbors, and some who had attended our wedding. Especially friends of mine who knew the truth about what had happened between us yet still, like me, remembered him with love and affection.

Many more showed up than I expected to see. Three weeks had passed since he had died — I had been home for Thanksgiving, comforted by family and friends there — and I had placed my announcement in the local paper. Old neighbors came, and some talked about what a happy, loving couple we had been. They chose pictures from that box of photos I had never taken to Marc, and one picked out one of the two of us, dancing at our wedding, saying, "This is how I will remember Marc. With Susan."

The greatest comfort for me was remembering Marc with Susan. Now that he was gone, I was free to let go of my disappointment with him and enjoy all the wonderful memories I had tried to put aside as I moved on with life. I could keep his photo out by the collection of his golf balls Alex had me take, golf balls from all of the places we had been together. Alex also gave me a bag of ashes, so I could leave some when I played a golf course we had really enjoyed. I had a wonderful afternoon at Pebble Beach where I walked out to the 18th tee with no one around on a glorious day and left a few ashes at a spectacular vista that Marc had loved, and then I went into the Lodge and toasted him with a glass of the most buttery Chardonnay on the menu. Days of tears over his final days finally gave way to appreciation for the time we had had, and great relief at having listened to no one's voice but my own as I stayed in my marriage and fought for longer than some might have thought I should.

As for RedTeeMan, I am ashamed to say that on the day I got the news about Marc, it occurred to me that I could leave him out of this. Wouldn't my grief be awkward for him? Couldn't I easily just not tell him?

This quickly passed because I knew the kind of intimacy I hoped for in a partnership could not justify such a big omission. He came over with arms full of flowers and magazines. What seemed to bother him was that he and Marc couldn't be more different, yet I loved Marc. "But, you're both good men," I pointed out. "So, if he was a good man, how could you want out of the marriage?" he said, shaking his head. "I don't get that." Spoken like the ultimate bachelor. Was he saying I was the one who could not wholly commit?

Over the months to come, RedTeeMan made no progress toward intimacy and commitment. Oh, he went into escrow on a house, but I never believed he was going to go through with the purchase. When his company was sold and he was out of a job, not only was there no suggestion of taking a break so that we could spend some time together, he announced, "We're going to have even less time together because I've got to work at pursuing other possibilities." He canceled his offer on the house.

CHAPTER TWENTY-ONE

Re-Match

RedTeeMan never did step up, not surprisingly really or even disappointingly. I started to notice inconsistencies in his stories about where he was going and where he had been, but the kicker came in June 2012 when he said he had to go out of town to see a newborn in his family. I laughed out loud — he was so not a "see the baby" kind of guy that I related this story to a friend over lunch.

"Is he still online?" she asked.

"Well, I don't know. I haven't even looked."

When I went home, I did a bit of searching on the big dating sites and found that he was now using a new code name on one of them. I typed the code name into Google and found him on two more dating sites, including one targeting people in relationships who want to cheat on their partner.

I picked up my phone and programmed it to send all of his calls right to voice-mail, and next time he called I emailed to tell him I'd had enough of the evasions, half-truths, and outright lies and would like him to leave me be.

He did, except for the occasional text or email, and I moved on optimistically in the hope of finding someone and something genuine. There were times when I felt I had wasted that yearlong mulligan on RedTeeMan, because my instincts that he was not one to share life had not been wrong, and I wondered why I'd had to wait until my instincts told me he was deceiving me to move on. If I cried over this at all, it was less about the loss than self-pity: I wondered if maybe it wasn't too late for me to find someone I'd enjoy the way I had enjoyed Marc.

I had my best round at Sharp Park that summer, 86 on our long and tough course, and then played well in the club championship to finish second by one stroke to defending champ Lisa. Of course I had my usual miserable rounds, too, but those successes reminded me that you keep putting the ball on the tee and smacking it and every now and then a little miracle happens. With disappointments in both love and business, I needed that reminder every Sunday on the golf course. I was working, but not for profit, and I was dating, but not with conviction.

I also could not afford to invest in what I was sure would be the best matchmaking service of all, a week at Bandon Dunes. This golf resort on the Oregon Coast had replaced Pebble Beach in the fantasies of golfers everywhere, and I had visited a couple of years earlier to compare the two golf paradises for an article in *GottaGoGolf*. Sometimes I think the builder was playing a joke on the female golfer as he installed

head-high facial mirrors in the showers (no bathtubs anywhere on the property) and opened a cigar bar with pool
tables in the lodge. A fitness room was in the basement,
right next door to the cigar bar. There was no spa, no pool,
nothing to do, really, except play golf a couple of times a day.
But the golf courses are glorious, and as I sat in the manly
leather-and-paneled dining room, there were men everywhere. For a time I was the only woman in the room! In
what I thought was a relationship with RedTeeMan at the
time, I met a lot of seemingly great guys who asked, "Wow,
how do I meet someone like you?" I drove off thinking, next
time I need Match.com, I'll sign up for Bandon instead.

Alas, on Christmas Eve 2012, I opted for a free service
over the more ideal but pricey setup. And there I was on
OKCupid, this time as "GolfWineDine" looking at a new
opponent..er..suitor.

> **I just wanted to say "hello"... "MsGolfWineDine"... I
> don't have any clever pickup lines. I really like your
> look. That you have an 18 handicap is amazing n an ab-
> solute turn on... I really don't like going back and forth
> with emails or texting, I like to meet. It's all about the
> chemistry. I'd love to play golf sometime, anywhere you
> choose.**

It was raining terribly and all the courses were under water! Even a golf slut has standards. When the efficient "click"
of club contacting ball sounds like "splat" and is followed by
"shit!" it is no longer golf.

But he was nice looking, and he loved golf, and though

he seemed to have punctuation issues occasionally he could put subject and verb together. Hmmm.

When a few weeks later he checked in again — during a dry period — I decided to check him out online. After all, he seemed to be using his real name. So I came across his past, which involved some serious professional, legal and ethical issues involving sex, apparently occurring during the course of his marriage.

I did more research. It seemed he had paid a price for his transgressions, and then rebuilt his career. I did my best Carrie Bradshaw and asked friends: Can't people redeem themselves? Isn't forgiveness an essential value? Hey, look, Tiger Woods is getting sponsors again. Couldn't I just go play golf with TransgressionMan and trust my gut?

Those who did not immediately shout NO looked at me strangely while saying nothing. Meanwhile, he kept on emailing me. I pointed out to him that the more OKCupid questions I answered that he had answered, the lower our MATCH rating dropped and the higher our ENEMY quotient rose. He discounted these numbers and said it was chemistry that mattered, while I said it was shared values that mattered and the fact that he didn't care about our common beliefs and values and I did indicated that we weren't a good match. Shouldn't we both just move on, I asked? Oh, let's play golf just to make sure, he answered.

The golf slut began to waver. Just golf, what could be the harm?

So I looked at his specific answers to some of the many

OKCupid questions. For instance: *Imagine that you come home to find a partner pouring red wine all over a stranger's naked body and then licking it off. Which, if any of the following, would bother you most?* The humorous options for answers included: "spilling red wine" or "that I wasn't invited." I checked "the cheating." He checked the other serious option: "actually, this would not bother me."

Here's another one: *Suppose a close friend's partner is very attractive and thinks you're attractive, too. If you could enjoy a few hours of sex with them and your friend would never find out about it, would you do it?* I checked "no." He checked "yes" and commented, "depends on the relationship."

He also stated that he would date someone just for the sex, had had sex with someone within the first hour of meeting her, is open to non-monogamous relationships, and, here's the one that had my brakes totally screeching: *Would you have sex with someone, if you were blindfolded and would never know who it was, only that it would be someone you had never met before?* Oh yes of course he would.

So much for redemption and rehabilitation. These were the very attitudes that had gotten him in trouble in the first place.

TransgressionMan really wanted to play golf and said he even taught golf part-time. I just couldn't do it. I saw the answers to these questions and saw infidelity written all over the place. I saw values I would never share. If I played golf with him and felt any kind of chemistry at all … well, after RedTeeMan, this is exactly the kind of time suck I was trying to avoid now.

It wasn't that I wasn't a golf slut anymore; to the contrary, I had become such a dedicated golf slut that I didn't want to be distracted by a man who represented trouble. Tears and heartbreak are not conducive to taking dead aim at a four-inch hole a few hundred yards away. I wanted a man who would be good for my game, not ruin it.

I also had become an educated golf slut, so I knew that I was not looking for a man who played golf, I was looking for a man who liked playing golf with a woman. All of my fam trips, where I was the only woman in a foursome or sometimes in the entire group, had taught me that some men just want to play with the guys. There was one fam where my foursome was about to tee off and the fellows were getting their wagers in order, quibbling about who would get how many strokes and from which tees. One I had played with the previous day said to another, "What about Susan? She can play, let's bring her in on the bets." And the other guy said, "Nah, she's a woman," blinking back at the guy as if he must not have noticed this. I found some consolation in that Mr. Man had a miserable day and I, left out of the bets, quietly played solidly. But, I understand his objection: he played a game where he hit a long ball off the tee and then could either find it and play a second shot into the green, or not find it and sort of fabricate the rest of the hole from there, and mentally give himself just two putts on the green so that when he blew his 12-footer six feet by the hole he gave himself the next one, none of which really seemed like golf as I know it. Meanwhile, he'd have to give me probably 10 strokes while I repeatedly striped the ball to the middle of the fairway, couldn't reach the green, chipped on, and then two-putted for bogey — none of which seemed like golf as he knew it. One guy on a fam trip told me quite bluntly, "I want to play with the guys I want to play with, and if we've got a woman in the group who is a 20 that messes things up." All the worse if she hates cigar smoke and the men feel compelled to curtail their curse-words. For some guys, golf is like that locker room to which I was often barred in my sports-writing career. Those are not the guys I wanted to find.

On New Year's Eve that year, it seemed my luck had changed. I had an unforgettable round of golf with a fellow golf slut from OKCupid who turned out to be one of the most honest men I have ever met. I'm calling him GameMan here because he not only had game, he was game. All those usual email hoops? Not for him — he quickly invited me to play golf at a course convenient to both of us.

It was such a cold morning that as I made it up the hill to the course my German car's bell chimed to tell me the temperature was below 40 degrees. But there was blond and blue-eyed GameMan, looking fit and friendly and just enough taller than me, and off we went for one of the most challenging rounds of golf I've ever played.

Not only did we wait quite a bit behind slow groups, we

sloshed through mud and spattered ourselves swinging on thin, soft lies. Neither of us played well, yet whining was minimal and we both stayed upbeat — I kind of gave him an out as we passed the clubhouse at one point, saying, "If it weren't for you I'd probably be heading inside right about now," but he kept on walking so I did too. (Turns out, he hadn't heard me.)

We also transcended the typical first-date small talk to share perspectives on why our marriages had failed and what kinds of experiences we'd been having on OKCupid. By the 15th hole we had skipped ahead to examine what it was we were really looking for. He seemed frustrated at not finding something potentially meaningful; I told him I was hoping to find someone special and if I kept meeting nice guys like him I eventually would.

As we sat exhausted over a 19th hole cocktail, it seemed we had both had a good time and would want to do this again — under warmer, dryer conditions. GameMan mentioned, however, that he and his wife were only separated. And in a later exchange of emails, he said he was not sure where they were headed and he knew I was looking for a partner, but would I mind a bit of hanky panky while I was looking?

Darn it!

We had a few emails of rational and funny discussion about this — "I don't want to fill up on appetizers when the next course could be a gourmet entree," I wrote — before he concluded that he had best be moving on.

Weeks later, I wrote GameMan to thank him for telling the truth, because soon I was having a grand time in a romance with a golf pro while also dating a super-nice executive I had met a few months earlier. Both were soon to fizzle and that was okay — the golf pro hated my swing, and the super-nice guy wouldn't schedule a golf date with me. (Okay, so maybe I oversimplify here.) But I appreciated that GameMan didn't waste my time (I guess so that I myself could instead waste my time with these other guys).

On the other hand, RedTeeMan would probably read this and say, "Hey, see, the honest guy doesn't get anywhere. It doesn't pay to tell the truth."

CHAPTER TWENTY-TWO

An Unplayable Lie

R edTeeMan texted me almost weekly when the Baltimore Ravens were making their Super Bowl run.

"Give me 10 points and I'll take the Colts. $20."

"I'll give you and the Ravens three points. $20."

I am such a loyal fan, I don't know how I managed to keep my fingers off the Swype keyboard of my smart phone. I know I dreamed up a smarty-pants retort or two that went to waste. At the very least, I thought I ought to tell him exactly how much money I had saved him by ignoring him. One little gloat, how could it hurt?

On Super Bowl Sunday it was particularly tempting. Clad in purple, I reported to Sharp Park to receive the mock outrage of my red-covered club mates rooting for their hometown Niners. At least, I think it was mock — but they were every bit San Francisco 49er fans as I was a Raven rooter. As I made my way around the course, I looked down at the golf ball and thought of Ray Lewis, the Ravens' tough linebacker who had declared this his last game. "Ray would

smack this ball," I'd tell myself. Or, "Ray wouldn't hold anything back."

Lewis had himself quite a past. After Super Bowl XXXIV
in Atlanta, he'd been a passenger in a limousine with two
friends who were charged in a double-murder following a
brawl outside a bar; after making his plea deal, he had become an exemplary member of the Baltimore community
through his nonprofit Ray Lewis 52 foundation, preaching
and quoting scripture all along. "No weapon formed against
us shall prosper," had become the battle cry of the Ravens
there at the end of Lewis' 16-year career. Some ridiculed
him; we Baltimore fans adored him but had come to do so in
good humor. When one of my 49er-fan golf companions
said, "But he's a murderer," I retorted with a mock snicker,
"Oh why do you have to bring up that old thing? We all have
SOMEthing in our past." Giggle, swing, what a putt, 92, and
please show me the money so I can get a nice bottle of
champagne to drink after the game.

I remained "dark" when it came to RedTeeMan, however.
I was at peace with my instincts months earlier and envisioned a contented life without any further contact. It was
over. I celebrated the Ravens' Super Bowl victory without a
word to him.

A few days later, an email from him popped into my inbox. It contained only a link, and I easily recognized it as a
spam virus. I'd made the mistake of opening a previous link,
also from his address, and passed the virus on to my entire
contact list, so this time my finger tapped the DELETE key

and I went on with my day.

But a few hours later, I noticed a reply-all to the spam from someone named Jane.

FIX YOUR EMAIL YOU CREEP, I HAD YOU BLOCKED AFTER THE SAMANTHA INCIDENT. HOW YOU COULD DO THAT TO HER IS BEYOND ME. TO THINK I KNEW YOU IS MY SHAME. GO TO HELL AND NEVER CONTACT ME AGAIN. I WILL BLOCK YOU ONCE AND FOR ALL.

It felt like I had been over RedTeeMan for a long time. Maybe since our first breakup. I don't think there would have been a second go-round if I had been thriving professionally and making other connections, and so it had been easy for me to move on from the second breakup. This email did not alarm me. It amused me, piqued my curiosity, and somehow validated my hard-reached conclusion.

But, who was Samantha? What had he done to her and when?

I replied, only to Jane.

I like your style! So, I dated RedTeeMan from Sept 09 until June 12, it took me that long to understand that he was a liar and a phony ... It would be most helpful to me to hear how he is a creep as I move along.

Jane forwarded this to some others. And the next night, this arrived:

This is Samantha. I dated him from 2009, until a couple of days ago. Apparently the same time you dated him. I

live in Atlanta. Yes, he is a liar and an unbelievable player. There are many of us.

Aha, so Samantha was the reason for all of those trips to "Coca-Cola" and maybe Home Depot and Aflac as well. (He didn't, she assured me later, have any business with the soda company or anyone else in Hotlanta, much as he longed for some.)

Jane, I would learn, lived in Seattle, where his supposed clients included a coffee brewer and department store.

They put me in touch with MJ, who had thought she was RedTeeMan's girlfriend a few years earlier until she got a call from a gal named Regina, who thought she was his girlfriend. Together, MJ said, they tracked down more than 20 women who were "dating" (at different levels) RedTeeMan at the same time they were. (This was during the same time he was supposedly engaged to his most recent fiancée.) And I traded emails with Annie, who lived not too far from me and had dated him at the same time I... and Samantha... and Jane did.

There indeed were many of us. I did not meet Layla from Las Vegas or Jeanie in San Diego or Sharon and Cindy and Liza from the Bay Area, or any of the many others that Jane and Samantha had discovered. (Sharon! No wonder he had called me by that name once or twice! A receptionist at work, he had said, rolling his eyes at his mistake. Oh, but maybe that part was true.) Samantha, who was on to him enough to inspect his phone once or twice while he took those many showers, guesses the number could be as high as 20 women at any one time — all of them smart, attractive, busy women, most of whom thought they were building a loving relationship with a solid, church-going businessman.

A man who said grace before meals, and believed in the devil.

No wonder RedTeeMan resisted comparison to the George Clooney character in *Up in the Air.* He no doubt felt much closer to the double-life-living female lead played by Vera Famiglia — times 10! No wonder he said he could not see what he had in common with my ex-husband — he knew he could not ever compare favorably with an honest man.

I thought it might be helpful if I sketched out for these women the relationship I had thought I had had, and so I put it all into a pithy 2,500 words. Samantha emailed me back in just a few minutes.

On the treadmill at the gym.....whew think I need to run an extra five miles.

When she got home, she wrote out her experience — so much like mine, starting with instant chemistry at a Match.com-precipitated meeting in Las Vegas exactly three months and a week before he met me. Glowing in the excitement of a new romance, she would never have imagined her suitor pursuing others with abandon, as he did me. How could he? I realized that while I was not feeling much yet beyond amusement, two years earlier I would have been devastated by this reveal. I called Samantha immediately and we spoke until our phones were about to peter out.

She had come to realize what he was in an earlier email debacle — the one referenced in the email from Jane. Apparently he had been eager to report that he was about to make an offer on a particular house, and accidentally sent the same email out to several women in CC, not the blind CC he surely intended to use, so they could see he wasn't just talking to them. But she kept taking him back because he convinced her that she was special. When she read my email, she got the impression that he had had almost the same relationship with me, and she vowed that it was over.

We went over some of the timing — my first Christmas Eve with him, he had been with her a few days before that. We don't really know where he went on Christmas Day.

That New Year's Eve, he really was watching his grandkids because he called us — Jane too — and put them on the phone.

Super Bowl weekend 2012, he and I had gone to the Ritz Carlton Half Moon Bay and played golf on my birthday with a couple from my golf club — "he's a keeper," my gal pal had told me approvingly. Then after a lazy, sumptuous brunch at the resort the next morning, we returned to my place to watch the game on my couch; throughout, Samantha said, he was texting her "from his CEO's party in Las Vegas" — "boring, but the food is good," he told her.

Of course he probably told me that his CEO was texting

him about something or other, and I, so awed by his work ethic, would easily believe him.

But he had spent two New Year's Eves with her, and escorted her for family weddings. Her house was full of photos of someone she never really knew and never wanted to see again. On the one hand, I admired that she had let him in to her life so completely — on the other, I felt grateful that I had limited his access to mine.

But, as she said, it didn't matter either way.

There was more, much of it pretty sickening. He had mastered techno-cheating, using phone and text and email — even Skype — to make himself available from anywhere. That trip to Japan when he was texting me several times a day — Jane and Samantha and who knows how many others also were getting texts (and gifts). Maybe he just copied and pasted everything! But, I never detected anything odd that seemed to be meant for someone else. Of course, now and then he swore that we had discussed something that I was sure we had not — but, at this age, that seems more normal than not. And there was that one night he had been away for a while and I suggested "Skype tonight?" When he answered "How about tomorrow night?" I got a little bit pissy. But the next day he told me that his phone and laptop had been taken from him overnight for a security check, and that sounded too outrageous to me to have been a lie. I think I even apologized for my attitude. Now, I can only admire the creativity of the story.

***

He was so smart, so much smarter than me. He probably could have been Barack Obama if he had not been so busy tracking and filing all of the idiosyncrasies of so many women around the country, juggling his schedule, planning his travel, concocting his lies.

He never reneged on a date we had made. He almost always showed up on time. Did he keep spreadsheets? A detailed calendar? No wonder he stayed up long into the night sending emails. No wonder he kept asking, "When is your birthday again?" No wonder my friends thought him distant — he could not take the chance that someone less trusting than me would see through his act.

Ah, now I finally knew what he had meant that time when he had said, "I thought you were probably tired of my act." It was all, from start to finish, an act. It became more sick the more I thought about the extent of his lies. That time I had been in Monterey and he wanted to know why I hadn't returned his calls — he probably had accidentally called one of the others! The conversations about Tiger Woods' chronic infidelity — what a kinship he must have felt, along with probably a smugness for not having gotten himself hitched to one woman who would clobber him with a golf club and cramp his style. All the weekends working out of town, where he'd text some very specific story about what he was doing that evening, and then have a charming anecdote if I happened to ask about it the next day.

It was one thing for a man to be a so-called player, not pretending sincerity and devotion and love but simply flirting his way through the field. This man pretended, even insisted he was seeking a committed relationship, and had for many years been pretending with many women at a time.

I thought about airing him out, telling him what he was, but of course he already knew. Certainly he had ammunition to defend himself with an attack, and I did not care to hear it. I thought about calling his mother, his daughter, his sisters — all of whom, when I thought back on it, had seemed oddly devoid of any sincere interest in me, and no wonder. Why would they bother? How could they keep track?

So other than the occasional heart-to-heart with Samantha and a pitch to publish the story in a national publication, I did nothing but move on. Or I should say, I tried to move on.

I was 55 now, and I couldn't help noticing that my profile on Match.com wasn't attracting a measurable fraction of the interest it had when I was 50 and 51. Then, I had been so full of hope; now, suspicion. Then, I was certain there was a partner for me. Now, it occurred to me that maybe love had passed me by while I was wasting my tee-times with RedTeeMan.

And what good were those hours on the course anyway? He had so mastered the art of deception that I could not recall seeing any clues about him when we played golf together.

Now I remembered how he would inexplicably seem to

have improved even when we hadn't played together for a few weeks. His whole shtick about joining me at the red tees because he missed me — maybe he used that on one of the other ladies, too, playing golf with her on weekends when he was supposedly at a conference in Washington D.C.

What did I know, really? Golf, my dependable, no-fail window into the human character, had let me down so grievously this time.

Of course even a normal, healthy, loving relationship like the one I have with golf has its challenges and setbacks. We get a little cocky sometimes, score a birdie or two, and then here comes the post-birdie blow-up. But it works the other way, too: we splash and three-putt to an 8 and then regroup and make par on the next hole. I've always found satisfaction in navigating the ponds and bunkers, on golf courses and figuratively. I love the opportunity presented by a monumental screw-up: learn and improve, or wallow. I don't wallow. I look at the horrible score I carded on the front nine and think, "I can improve on that by 10 shots on the back nine and end up with a respectable score for the day."

The life metaphor wasn't holding up this time, however. This misjudgment of RedTeeMan felt bigger than any bad round of golf, and made so much less sense. I felt a nagging impulse to go to Bodega Bay and scatter some of Marc's ashes at the seventh tee and let go — but, let go of what? Let go of the belief that I would be able to share golf and love again with someone? Let go of the conviction that people tend to be sincere and kind? Let go of my bad memories of Marc, my good ones, all of them?

After the revelation of RedTeeMan and other disappointments — *GottaGoGolf* had exhausted my savings and now I was doing consulting and freelance work just trying to keep its name out there — I eyeballed my wedding anniversary on the calendar. May 19 was a Sunday. I could drive through the town of Two Rock past the cows Marc used to honk at, play an afternoon round at the course where we were married that day 13 years earlier, hear the seals bark in the distance, have a glass of wine on a sunny (or foggy) deck at the harbor. If I went there and did these things, maybe someday I would be able to go back. And maybe now I would be able to go forward.

Then an email came. Not a spam.

The Oakland City Championship. Net division for women. Two days, May 18 and 19.

I could go perform some personal last rites (that might serve no purpose after all). Or I could play golf. On the golf course where Marc and I had our first date and on the day we had been married.

I sent in my entry.

CHAPTER TWENTY-THREE

The Golf Gods Giveth...

On March 20, the first day of spring and the day that Marc and I had met 16 years earlier, I was schlepping my golf clubs and leading my parents through the airport in Baltimore. I had brought the clubs with me four days ago and still not used them; now, we were heading for Charleston, South Carolina, where we had rented a house at Isle of Palms for the whole family to gather and celebrate my father's 80th birthday. I would get out for a round one morning, I figured, and be ready for a special day at Kiawah Island's Ocean Course, where my brother Bob had been added to the guest list with me.

My dad and my mom, 78, were still playing golf as regularly as they could withstand Baltimore's weather whimsy. Mom had started playing when she was around 60, just to add another sport to the list she'd conquered. A jock before the days when it was fashionable for girls to be athletic, she'd excelled best at tennis and I always hated the way she would run me around the court chasing after her cagily placed shots. At 78, she still played in a tennis league. Golf she found much harder, but she joined a women's group and would become the last on the list to make the excuses "it's too hot" or "it's too cold" or "it's supposed to rain." Dad for a long time had a regular group of guys he played with, but health problems started to diminish their numbers. The last time I had visited them, my father sat out golf and I played with Mom, Bob, and his girlfriend, using Dad's clubs. His sticks amounted to nothing more than pieces of metal; they were the worst clubs I had ever used, and the grips offered no more traction than the metal itself. I asked, but he did not remember ever regripping them.

"Dad, you play enough golf, why don't you splurge on some new clubs?" I said, knowing that he and my mom still tried to walk nine holes regularly together. "The technology is so much better these days."

"I don't know how much longer I'll be able to play. I'm not sure it's worth it."

"Well, how about a real putter? The thing you have, it flaps around as soon as it makes contact with the ball. Surely you could save yourself some strokes there."

He seemed to agree. But I could not afford to completely re-arm him, so I went on eBay and selected a very well-priced senior set of irons and hybrids, asking that they be shipped without my name attached. They were there in the living room when I arrived, and though he had admired them he had not gotten to try them yet. It was raining and cold.

I had brought my own clubs in order to break 100 at Kiawah, but when I picked up my brother at the Charleston airport later that night, I noticed he had not brought his.

"I couldn't change my flight," he said. "I don't know if I'll play on Monday."

This offended my golf slut sensibilities. A free round at the Ocean Course? A once in a lifetime opportunity. He had no idea, obviously, or he'd rent a car and drive the 570 miles back to Baltimore after the round.

Our weekend weather was not good, with wind and rain sending us to the couch to watch the NCAA Tournament. Basketball game after basketball game — it seemed appropriate for my dad, who loved the game and even timed his retirement so that it was right before March Madness. My brother Tom brought his harmonica and guitar and made some music with brother Carl's budding musician son, but otherwise it was a very mellow party.

And then, so much for mellow. Everyone left on Sunday except my parents, and the wind was howling when I drove them to the airport on Monday morning. I had spent a week with them now and had seen how difficult things had become for them. My father had been the victim of a phone scam targeting seniors that week while I was sitting there in his living room. He immediately realized his mistake and got off the phone, but on the advice of the state's fraud prevention agency went straight to the bank to close his account.

He also feared that people were coming into his third-floor condo when he was not there, and fretted uncertainly about decisions and directions in ways he never had.

I saw my mother finding ways to help him adjust to such changes without insulting or patronizing him. Instead of impatiently saying, "You just missed our exit," she was learning to pay attention and helpfully say, "Isn't this where we usually turn?" I tried to follow her example, but by the time they headed home I was exhausted from the effort not to sound like a know-it-all, and I worried about them. As I drove to Kiawah Island and heard the reports of gale winds, I breathed easier. This, I thought, would be so much more surmountable than my parents' struggle with aging.

The Ocean Course parking lot was empty. The crazy winds had sidelined almost all of the golfers — not just my brother, but my friend at the resort who had joined me twice before. "I know you can play there any time, so please don't feel you have to come out in these conditions," I had emailed. He thanked me and said indeed, he did not think his game was up to the challenge.

But there was the smiling face of the caddie I had again requested. David introduced me to my companion for the day, Dave from the state of Washington, and I stopped in the pro shop to say hello.

Head professional Stephen Youngner said with a smile I was about to experience the Ocean Course in all its glory, or fury, however I preferred to look at it. A day this windy was as rare as a day perfectly calm — most days were somewhere in between.

Fortunately, David and Dave embraced the spirit of the day. Battened down in our jackets and our watch caps — I even had gloves on — we all agreed we were out to have a good time, and so we waived the Rules of Golf to the extent that we weren't going to hit out of any ridiculous lies or spend time searching for lost balls. (David has a knack for finding replacements along the way anyway, so I didn't worry when I lost a couple of balls early.) It was challenge enough to try to hit a 150-yard club into the wind to a green 100 yards away and get the ball to stop anywhere near the hole. On one par-3 I was proud to be on in one, yet lucky to four-putt for a 5.

As we completed the first four holes, all playing with the wind behind us, David remarked, "This is my hardest job as a caddie, to keep a guest upbeat through these next nine holes when they're playing into the wind." After 13, we would again turn our backs on the wind for the final five holes.

There could be no wondering whether Mom and Dad had made it home okay, no mapping out a catch-up work plan for the rest of the week, no speculating on why the man I'd been dating hadn't called or texted while I was gone. Aside from lively catch-up conversation with David, a positive force for both my game and my enjoyment, golf demanded complete engrossment.

I felt relief.

Then we were joined by the player behind us — David from Washington D.C. — and his caddie Dave. What a hoot, Susan and the four Davids. Where was Michelangelo?

I did not break 100 that day. But taking on the Ocean Course in conditions that had scared away all but the Daves exhilarated me. I was living life. And I was not ashamed to be a golf slut. I was proud.

Golf began wooing me back. I saw an email pop into my inbox from a high school boyfriend. Momentarily afraid to open it because I thought it might be from prison, I was touched to read about what he had made of himself and how he remembered me and my family, and how he had come across my website while doing a search on his two passions, golf and wine.

I made a new friend in whom I spotted more than just a glimmer of competitive spirit, and began golfing with her and her husband.

I made a point of joining my *GottaGoGolf* copy chief pal for occasional rounds in his retirement community, where one day walking off the first green I spotted a woman marshal and read the name on her cart: Betty Cuniberti, who had inspired me so many years ago, when I was in college and she was at the *Washington Star*, to become a sportswriter.

In a round of golf arranged by a friend, I met a woman whose business mind and golf passion would inspire me to revive the digital magazine concept of *GottaGoGolf*.

And at the encouragement of a former colleague from the

Chronicle, I began volunteering with The First Tee of Oakland, once a week playing with school kids who were learning a little bit of golf along with nine core values I realized the game had taught me, too. Most weeks I would go home exhausted but chuckling, especially the time the coordinator asked the kids, "What's more important in golf, hitting the ball into the hole or hitting it farther?" This group of 7-to-11-year-olds did not miss a beat, shouting, "FARTHER!" The coordinator was laughing too hard to muster a convincing argument to the contrary.

I hadn't forgiven golf yet for failing to expose RedTeeMan in some on-course test of character, and I saw no sense in seeking out golf dates that I no longer felt certain would tell me everything I needed to know about a man. Still, I was playing twice most weeks by the time the big tournament came up in May. The game made sense to me at a time when so many things did not.

Lisa, the reigning Sharp Park Business Women's Golf Club champion, had not played Lake Chabot and suggested a practice round with me the day before the tournament started, so we contestants would know what we were in for.

Lake Chabot is a hardly walkable, up-and-down municipal course in the tree-covered, turkey-populated hills above the Oakland Zoo that opened in 1923. There's no good reason for the name — only in one place, just past the ninth tee, can players who know where to look through the trees see the lake off in the distance. The course itself has no lakes or ponds, although it fell into such disrepair in the 1990s that big pools of water would appear on low spots in rainy season. There were rumors that the city was going to sell the course to the owners of a fancy resort nearby so that they could turn it into a private club, but those rumors died with the dot-com bomb. Instead, it closed for a couple of years for renovations to eradicate impromptu ponds and grow grass, and a management company came in to revive business.

By 2013, Lake Chabot was manned by the friendliest golf course staff in the Bay Area. Womanned too — with the golf-savvy proprietress of the concessions bound to know your name by the second time you stopped by her Shack. Oh, a lot of courses offhandedly call their snack stand "the shack," but at Chabot, the name applies in capital letters.

Arrival at the golf course offers an immediate drill in course management. Pass through the stone posts at the entry and then you are in the middle of the golf course, in your car, cutting through the middle of the fifth hole (check the tee uphill to your right before proceeding), the fourth hole (a safe crossing unless someone is ready to hit off the fairway to your left), the third hole (a safe crossing unless someone's tee shot from uphill right is crossing the road), the 11th hole (if it's early, nobody's here yet), then a stop sign. Here you've got to peek around the fence to the left to see if anyone is teeing off to the par-3 second green, which is on the right side of the road. No? Step on it, and then park at the first strip of dirt because it's right next to that unique par-6 hole that marks the end of your round.

It is 644 yards at the forward tees, starting with a drive that must start down the right side of the tree-lined fairway because left is OB and everything feeds there. Your next shot just needs to advance to a position where your third shot will make it to the bottom of the steep hill, so that your fourth shot has a good lie to make it up the final steep hill to the tiered green, where players so deeply fear going long that they often come up short.

That hole alone will stop most players from trying to walk the course. When I did, I was told I was one of very few women to walk and carry her golf bag at Lake Chabot. Then I stopped carrying my golf bag when I played, because I read some research that concluded walking-carrying burns only a few more calories than walking-pushcarting and is not as good for your score. It is impossible, however, to expeditiously traverse Chabot's par-3 ninth, which is 139 yards straight downhill and so plays about 110. One can walk down that hill at her peril, following a seldom used path without room for a pushcart, or take the cart path through the woods, which is a scenic route for a motor but quite a detour for a walker.

Are we tired yet?

Lisa and I rode together with a couple of older gentlemen, she playing a serious, score-keeping game and me taking replays and practicing putts where time allowed. I just didn't want a score in my head the next day, didn't want to be thinking, wow, yesterday I made 8 here, hope I don't do that again. I didn't want my putting in my head either, didn't want to be thinking, I missed all my four-footers yesterday, hope I don't do that again. My rationale that day was: don't take any four-footers, then you won't miss any. The greens, tiny as they are, were quick with breaks that appeared subtle and turned out to be sharp. On such fast and tiny greens, I decided, I would have to approach with a lob wedge that flew high and landed softly, Phil Mickelson style. (On the other hand, I tried a running sand wedge shot on the 14th green because the pin was in the back, and it found the hole for a birdie. Which made the hole with the San Francisco Bay view, 15, all the more scenic.)

Lisa and I talked strategy and rules, and I think we both went home and did some research. I was going to ride the next day with my new golf friend, Buffy, whom I had invited to enter. She had not played Chabot, and golf forbids giving advice to a fellow competitor, so I needed to know what constituted advice — to follow the Rules, of course, but also to be respectful of the third player in our group. I couldn't tell Buffy what club to use or that a hole played shorter or longer than its distance, but it was okay to tell her about the course and point out features. It turned out that our third, Diane, was a skilled and regular player at Chabot who helped us follow proper dropping procedures and seemed to enjoy talking through various rules scenarios.

As I reviewed such things the night before the tournament, I gave some thought to the challenge of deciding when to call a penalty on a fellow competitor. It wasn't a thing I would do unless the violation was intentional and considerable, amounting to cheating.

During the night I woke up with penalty calls still rattling around in my brain. And I started thinking, the thing about golf is that we call our own penalties. It's a game of integrity. RedTeeMan played as little golf as he thought he could to still keep me on his roster. He didn't really like golf. He wasn't a golfer. And so I learned nothing about him by playing golf with him. My character test proved useless with a nongolfer who was faking an interest in the game.

Ah. It wasn't golf's fault I had wasted time on RedTeeMan. He so excelled at phoniness everywhere he went, golf was not going to reveal his character. The game too had been fooled. And if the game I respected had been fooled, no wonder the rest of us, too, had failed to see through the façades, however many there had been, carefully maintained by a master manipulator.

This settled, I went back to sleep. I had forgiven my game and myself, and made peace.

The next morning, my game welcomed me back with a stunning score. "WOW!" That's what I said aloud when I added up my front nine after making par on that downhill par-3 ninth. My companions were struggling, but I had had all pars and bogeys except for one double. 43. I could break 90, something I had never done on this golf course. And I was getting 21 strokes! On the 14th hole, with San Francisco visible in the distance, I eyeballed a putt of 35 or 40 feet and said aloud, "I can see this going in." It did. That's the kind of day I had. All the putts I hadn't bothered to practice the day before landed in the cup.

I shot 87 and took a five-shot lead in the tournament with a net 66. I heard others looking at the scoreboard and asking, "Who is she?" The second-place player was a 16-handicapper, meaning she actually trailed me by 10.

That night, I took Marc's picture out and looked at the slogans on the decorative golf frame.

"When in doubt, hit the links... Live for the hole in one... The search for a perfect stroke is a lifetime challenge."

The search for the perfect anything is a lifetime challenge, yet we had had so many perfect days together. I could be forever grateful that they had come or forever miserable that they had gone, and I knew which choice I would make.

Finally I packed some of his ashes in a pretty sack and stowed them in my golf bag, thinking of scenic spots at Lake Chabot where he might like them scattered. And the next morning, no longer remembering that it was the 13th anniversary of my wedding, I teed off without the slightest stirring of a butterfly on the straightforward par-4 first hole.

It took me five shots just to reach the green at the crest of the hill. No worries, I thought, the green is tiny and I'm probably no more than 15 or 16 feet away. I'll take my 7 and move on.

Except, my first putt came up short. My second putt blew by the hole. My third putt missed and my fourth putt... Oh, I just can't remember it all now. Who five-putts a little green like that one? But that's what I did, rolling my eyes at the heavens where the golf gods surely giggled smugly. And now the butterflies started to roar as a 10 went in the first box on my scorecard.

In golf, there is really no such thing as a perfect 10.

My companions, Diane from the day before and now Carrie, checked their lipstick to be sure they looked presentable enough to accept a trophy. My mouth, meanwhile, was utterly saliva-less. I had to laugh. Where was the drink cart? At some other course, not Oakland's people's Chabot.

I made a 3 on the road-crossing second, but now I embarked on a battle with my brain. Nerves and adrenalin were not my friends, and while "don't think" worked as a line in a Woody Allen movie, I might as well have told myself not to breathe.

So, I gave in, and I thought. I calculated the closeness of my lower-handicapped and more-skilled companions, mapped out which holes I might conquer, and kept a dogged, one-shot-at-a-time determination to do my best with a smile. On some level, I conceded. I did not surrender, but I had to admit to myself, "I'm a 21-handicapper who had had a fairytale round to take the lead, and today the ride has turned back into a pumpkin." There wasn't any shame in succeeding wildly one day and failing the next. The point was to keep playing, to keep trying, to embrace the challenge.

Mentally, I rehearsed graciously shaking the hand of the winner, whoever she was. Up ahead of us, one of the women in our flight made a hole-in-one alongside The Shack at 12. Maybe it would be her. Maybe Carrie, who had such beautiful touch around the greens. She made a clutch putt on 17 for a bogey, but I made mine from the other side of the hole from about the same distance.

On to the last. I walked off the green with a 9 on 18, 100 on the day, head high, sure I had not won. Carrie had three-putted for an 8, 90 on the day. By now, I had given up on the complicated calculations and had no idea where any of us stood.

"I needed to beat you by 11 just to tie," she told me.

Said Diane, shaking her head at us, "Somebody else must have had a good day."

I like to say that the golf gods giveth and the golf gods taketh away. That drive you sent careening into the woods ricochets off a branch at just the precise angle that allows it to drop into the middle of the fairway 100 yards short of the hole, and the golf gods giveth. The perfect par putt makes a 360-degree turn at the hole and does not go in as the golf gods taketh. Usually, they're too subtle to do their giving and taking on a single hole; in my case, they had done it on consecutive days and to the extreme. I was a *Wide World of Sports* commercial for the thrill of victory and the agony of defeat in two disparate rounds of golf.

In the cool, quiet clubhouse, there was a hole-in-one to be celebrated, and so I joined the wide circle of women trading notes on the day. Other than for the single flawless shot, there was no flush of excitement from a player who thought she might have caught me.

My day had been just good enough, it became clear as the third-place and second-place names were announced and only mine remained. And as I gratefully took the small but heavy glass trophy into my shaking hands, new middle-aged champion at the local muni, I realized I hadn't thought of Marc on this journey. Oh, there might have been that moment on the first green when I rolled my eyes at the skies and wondered, "Is this your idea of a joke?" But once I buckled in for that bumpy ride, I had to keep my brain fixated on the horizon just to keep from throwing up. And I succeeded.

In the end, his ashes were still in my golf bag. I decided that's a perfectly fine place for them to stay.

CHAPTER TWENTY-FOUR

My Last Confession

Craigslist > Strictly Platonic > w4m

Just Golf (55)

I am a tall, good-looking and fun blonde who has given
up on dating sites but still would like to play golf with
men. (Actually just one at a time please -- and please be
single, unless you have a permission slip from your wife
or significant other. Golf is hard enough without being
chased around by angry women.) My index just went up
to 19.7 but I am basically a bogey golfer. In social golf, I
believe in one mulligan per nine and gimmes inside the
leather. I like the Oakland courses, Monarch Bay, Alameda, Sharp Park, Willow Park, and, for special occasions, Wente and Presidio and Hiddenbrooke and Half
Moon Bay. Open for Saturday mornings or the occasional weekday afternoon nine or 18. Game? You're on
the tee!

ACKNOWLEDGEMENTS

The story of RedTeeMan was first told in the essay The Power of Spam. *Thanks to Kristin Huckshorn, Regan McMahon, and Meredith White for their suggestions on making that incredible story more believable. Also thanks to the many friends who read* The Power of Spam *and responded, "UGH!"*

Thanks to Brooke Warner for giving this book its first professional critique, and to Richard Ayres for his patient crafting of the cover.

Thanks to Olga Stamatiou for conceptualizing and creating the beautiful painting 19th Hole, *which portrays the golf slut so elegantly that it was far too high-brow for the cover of this book.*

Finally, I am beyond grateful to have former colleagues and friends well-versed in taste, word choice, grammar, and the serial comma. Thank you Cori Brett, Bill Burnett, Kerry Kendall, Pat Sullivan, and Lesley Visser for your gentle touch and generous expertise. Extra thank-yous to Cori and Bill for all of the joyous days we have shared on golf courses, and to Emmy Moore Minister for her friendship and that one very special secret round.

ABOUT SUSAN FORNOFF
AND GOTTAGOGOLF

Susan Fornoff covered the Oakland A's for the *Sacramento Bee,* and other teams for *USA Today* and the *Baltimore News American,* in the early years of women sports-writers having access to locker rooms. When she took up golf in 1993, it seemed to her that the game had access issues for women players. Her GottaGoGolf media company continues to offer a fun, lively voice on behalf of golf for all.

For a Reading Group Guide or to make a Golf Slut Guest post, please visit **www.GottaGoGolf.com/blog.**

CPSIA information can be obtained at www.ICGtesting.com
Printed in the USA
LVOW13s1716090514

385158LV00006B/746/P